Helping Hyperactive Kids –
A Sensory Integration Approach

Helping Hyperactive Kids– A Sensory Integration Approach

Techniques and Tips for Parents and Professionals

Lynn Horowitz, MHS, OT
Cecile Röst, PT

Hunter House PUBLISHERS

Hunter House Inc., Publishers
PO Box 2914
Alameda CA 94501-0914

Library of Congress Cataloging-in-Publication Data
Horowitz, Lynn.
Helping hyperactive kids : a sensory integration approach /
Lynn Horowitz and Cecile Röst. — 1st ed.   p. cm.
Originally published as: Help, een druk kind! / Cecile Röst en Lynn Horowitz.
Reed Business Information, 2004.
Includes bibliographical references and index.
Translated from the Dutch, with rev. and new material in English from the original work.
ISBN-13: 978-0-89793-481-7
ISBN-10: 0-89793-481-4
1. Attention-deficit-disordered children. 2. Hyperactive children. 3. Senses and sensation in chil-
dren. I. Röst, Cecile C. M. II. Röst, Cecile C. M. Help, een druk kind! English. III. Title.
[DNLM: 1. Attention Deficit Disorder with Hyperactivity—psychology. 2. Attention Deficit Dis-
order with Hyperactivity—therapy. 3. Child. 4. Occupational Therapy—methods. 5. Physical
Stimulation. 6. Sensation. WS 350.8.A8 H816h 2006a]
RJ506.H9H67 2006
618.92'8589—dc22   2006020905

Project Credits

Cover Design	Peri Poloni-Gabriel
Book Production	John McKercher
Illustrator	Rinkje Wal
Translator	Joan MacDonald
Developmental and Copy Editor	Jude Berman
Proofreader	John David Marion
Indexer	Nancy D. Peterson
Translation Editor	Lynn Horowitz
Acquisitions Editor	Jeanne Brondino
Editor	Alexandra Mummery
Senior Marketing Associate	Reina Santana
Rights Coordinator	Candace Groskreutz
Customer Service Manager	Christina Sverdrup
Order Fulfillment	Washul Lakdhon
Administrator	Theresa Nelson
Computer Support	Peter Eichelberger
Publisher	Kiran S. Rana

Printed and bound by Bang Printing, Brainerd, Minnesota
Manufactured in the United States of America

9 8 7 6 5 4 3   First U.S. Edition   12 13 14 15 16

Contents

Preface

Lynn Horowitz has been an occupational therapist since 1969 and has been involved with sensory integration (SI) since the beginning of her career. In 1973, she established a successful private practice specializing in SI therapy in Atlanta, Georgia—the first such practice in that state. Her life then took her to Israel, where she introduced SI through small educational sessions and taught a course in reflex development at Hebrew University. She returned to the United States, where she conducted research and received a master's degree from the University of Florida. Her last position in America was as an adjunct professor at the University of North Carolina at Chapel Hill, where she set up a course in anatomy and physiology for a new occupational therapy master's program and served as a consultant to the State Education Department. Lynn's goal in returning to school was to determine how SI therapy affects eye movements and organizational time. After completing her degree, she moved to the Netherlands and continued to pursue this research, while working with Professor W. R. A. Oosterveld at the Amsterdam Medical Center. Lynn was the director of a large SI educational service in the Netherlands for twenty-two years and established a multidisciplinary private practice there. She now resides in Cozumel, Mexico, working part-time in a rehabilitation center, writing the next book on motor planning, and finishing her research on motor observations.

I met Lynn Horowitz in 1988. After I received training in physiotherapy, I wanted to work with children, so I went to Pakistan and Germany, two countries where I did not need further training to work as a physiotherapist with children. These experiences led me to study SI therapy with Lynn. A new world opened up for me. I learned from Lynn and her professors and teachers how I could transform complicated neurological theories into play-based therapy. The children enjoyed the treatment so much they did not want to go home. The results were remarkably positive. In the beginning, I thought it might be a coincidence that the children's behavior and motor skills improved so significantly. After years of therapy experience, I came to realize that the improvements were not coincidental, but rather were more or less predictable, and that their inception could be linked to the beginning of therapy.

In the meantime, I had three school-age children of my own and acquired fourteen years of work experience, including training in neurological development methods, orthopedic methods in physiotherapy, and chiropractic methods. I found many opportunities to use the ideas of SI exist within the therapeutic arena and also within the educational realm. Therapists and teachers who are open to this approach find they can assist with issues they are normally able to address only through more traditional means.

One reason to try SI therapy is because children and adults find it a pleasurable form of therapy. The activities are neither too easy nor too difficult and everyone is able to encounter his or her own personal challenge. This is one of the basic ideas put forth by Dr. A. Jean Ayres, the founder of SI therapy. The therapist leads the client by helping him or her follow an inner, individual drive to achieve. In this manner, the therapist can employ a therapeutic yet playful way to improve motor and sensory skills, which in turn can change behavior. The art lies in understanding how the therapist and client can begin the process in a playful and friendly way.

Lynn and I wanted to write this book to provide more information about the SI approach for parents and therapists working with hyperactive children. We believe parents and professionals who have good information can be the best advocates for their children. In the Netherlands, more than 5,000 of the SI brochures we wrote for parents were sold over a twenty-year period.[1] We realized this indicated the need for a more up-to-date book—not only for parents, but also for therapists interested in or trained in SI. Because we were concerned that doctors in the Netherlands might be incorrectly diagnosing many children as hyperactive, we thought this situation deserved attention from a new angle. We wanted to offer an alternative to medical intervention. The result was *Help, een druk kind*, which was published in the Netherlands in 2004. This new edition is a translation of that book, with additional and updated material included specifically for the English-speaking audience.

SI theory and therapy originally was developed by Dr. A. J. Ayres in California. Her neuroscience work there supported her scientific findings and her test batteries. We are happy that our California-based publisher is now bringing this information back to the United States and other English-speaking countries.

We dedicate this book to Dr. A. J. Ayres.

DEDICATION

———◆·◆———

This book is dedicated to all the children and adults who have trusted me; to all the teachers, colleagues, and helpers with whom I have worked so many years; and to my wonderful husband and children who make it possible for me to immerse myself in my work. I give warm thanks to the children in my therapy. Their affection, their sincerity, their hyperactivity, their calm, their reclusive nature, their secrets, and their shortcomings have all enriched my life.

— *Cecile Röst*

I dedicate this book to my parents and my two stepchildren. My mother went through so much with me. I was her firstborn—hypersensitive as a baby, as a toddler, and for the rest of my life. Since my career as a therapist began, it has been my goal to help parents deal with their "problem children" in a compassionate and friendly way. I have learned a great deal from my very special children. I also dedicate this book to Dr. A. Jean Ayres who has started so many therapists on the road to helping children and adults with her special approach. Her compassion and careful scientific research have provided a theoretical basis for sensory integration. Children and adults throughout the whole world have been helped by this approach.

— *Lynn Horowitz*

Acknowledgments

Many thanks to the parents who helped us write this book by reading the manuscript, making comments, and contributing stories about their children. Many of these stories have been included in this book as examples. The names of the children involved have been changed.

We are also indebted to the colleagues who read the contents of this book with a critical eye. Thanks to their editorial and professional expertise, the book became clearer and more readable to a nonclinical audience as well as professionals.

Important Note

The material in this book is intended to provide a review of resources and information related to helping hyperactive children. Every effort has been made to provide accurate and dependable information. However, professionals in the field may have differing opinions, and new research may lead to changes in theory. Any of the treatments described herein should be undertaken only under the guidance of a licensed health-care practitioner. The authors, editors, and publishers cannot be held responsible for any error, omission, professional disagreement, outdated material, or adverse outcomes that derive from use of any of the treatments or information resources in this book, either in a program of self-care or under the care of a licensed practitioner.

Chapter 1

Why This Book?

A nice child, but he never sits still.

IN THIS CHAPTER, we introduce the basic approach of sensory integration (SI) and look at how it applies to hyperactive children. You may be wondering, for example, whether your child's hyperactive behavior is deliberate. Are there reasons for this disorder? How does SI processing take place? What does an SI evaluation include? What is SI therapy like? We will address these and related questions as we explain in an easily understandable manner the role of processing stimuli and its effects on a child's behavior.

To the Parents

This book was written to help you as a parent. If you are the parent of a hyperactive child, it is meant to serve as a resource and guide for you. We explain how the development of your child can be encouraged in a playful way, using the SI approach. We also discuss how parenting can become more enjoyable as you try some of the techniques in this book and experiment with viewing your child from a perspective that might be somewhat different from your current view.

Better Understanding

We often hear questions such as, "Why does my child behave this way?" "Is it my fault?" "Have I done something wrong?"

Implicit in these questions is the suggestion that the answers will lead to an affirmation that the child's behavior has been caused by something the parent has or has not done. We have chosen to view this problem and its solution from a different angle. By considering the underlying causes of their children's behavior, parents can move away from self-recrimination and toward helping their children fulfill their individual potential.

Our purpose is to provide insight into the behavior of your child. We want to help you better understand your hyperactive child. This understanding can be of benefit to your child as well as to you as the parent and to any others who come into direct contact with these often challenging, high-energy children. Using the techniques described in this book, parents, helpers, and educators can find interaction with these special children more pleasurable.

Every child is unique and develops his or her own way of approaching the world. For this reason, this is not a recipe book. It is far more than just a collection of practical tips to help a hyperactive child process stimuli in a better way. By considering and applying the suggestions presented in this book, you will also gain a better understanding of the physiological processes involved in the development of hyperactive behaviors.

Dealing with Unconscious Behavior

The behavior of children who are, for example, very active, inattentive, impulsive, impatient, or very loud, is often deemed as suspect and considered inappropriate, even "bad." Companions, helpers, and parents often think these children have more conscious control over their behavior than they actually have.[1] If your child is inattentive, you might say, "Kristin just won't pay attention" or "Matthew just wants to play; he's always on the go" or "Jeff is too lazy to pay attention." And yet Kristin, Matthew, and Jeff do want to pay attention—*they just can't.* Even if they try their hardest to do so, they just can't.

Sometimes a child's behavioral problem has a psychological or educational cause. In other cases, the child may have a problem processing certain stimuli. The problem may not be psychologically or educationally based, but rather the result of unconscious factors. SI-trained therapists can evaluate these factors and get to the root of the problem.[2]

A Different Approach

The medical approach to children's behavioral problems involves prescribing medication as a way of helping children focus. Medication is generally administered in a dose that allows the child to concentrate well during school hours. This approach has become very popular, especially among parents who do not object to giving these medications to their children. Ritalin is the most frequently prescribed medical intervention in the United States and the Netherlands. In fact, for some children, medication can resolve certain aspects of the problem quite quickly.

As a result of many years of providing SI therapeutic intervention, we learned that each child has different needs. Some parents whose children are receiving medication also wish to obtain behavioral advice about how to improve their children's situation and behavior at home. In this case, SI therapy can be used as a supplemental form of treatment. Other parents want their children to have SI therapy instead of a medical intervention; in this case, SI therapy serves as a different approach. Either way, it is important to remember that your child's unique therapy needs must be met.

Sensory Integration

We use the letters *SI* to stand for *sensory integration*. This refers to the processing of information that our eyes, ears, skin, muscles, joints, mouth, nose, and sense of balance deliver to the brain. This processing takes place in various sensory systems. One example is the visual system. Besides the eyes, the visual system includes the optical nerves and their connections, as well as the part of the brain that processes visual information. The whole system is involved in the process of seeing.

Babies, toddlers, preschoolers, and young children are constantly busy discovering their own bodies and trying to figure out how to use them. Every nerve receives specific stimuli to process. But what is most amazing is that all the information from the different nerves is integrated so that an image can be produced in the brain. Our nerves work together to coordinate and correctly route the information. This cooperation is what we call *sensory integration*.[3]

For example, imagine that Patrick wants to put on his hat. What has to *happen?*

- Patrick uses his eyes to look at the hat.
- Patrick uses his muscles and joints to feel exactly where his hat is.
- As he moves his arm up and toward his hat, his automatic balance reactions help him adjust.

(cont'd.)

- His sense of touch tells him he is holding the front of the hat with his fingers.
- Muscles and joints detect that he has firmly clasped the hat in his fingers. He moves the hat upward and places it on his head (motor planning).
- Patrick's sense of touch lets him know that the hat sits firmly on his head.
- Muscles and joints in his neck register the difference in weight and adapt to the new situation. He has done it! He has put on his hat!

How your child learns to relate to his or her environment depends on your child's ability to absorb, process, and respond to environmental stimuli. For your child to develop optimal motor, emotional, and social skills, it is necessary for all the sensory systems to function well. It is important that all the information streaming in from different systems be coordinated and successfully integrated.

Sensory Integration Therapy

Sensory integration therapy, also known as *SI therapy*, is a method of treating children who have problems processing sensory stimuli, called *sensory integration disorders*. It focuses on improving the child's capacity for integrating sensory input. It is very important to treat a child with this type of disorder in a positive way.[4]

Your child has to be encouraged to do what he or she is capable of doing and needs to be given just the right challenge."[5] The therapist must be careful to organize the setting and material so your child feels a sense of accomplishment and can say, "I did it!" This feeling of success is an important first step in your child's ability to process sensory stimuli.

SI therapy can be useful in dealing with problems such as learning difficulties, motor problems, dyspraxia, behavioral difficulties, anxiety disorders, autism, hemiplegia (spastic muscles primarily on one side of the body), and whiplash. In this book, SI therapy is only described with respect to how it relates to *hyperactive* children. According to National Institute of Mental Health statistics from 2003, three to five percent of school-age children in the United States show signs of hyperactivity. Thus, if a classroom has twenty-five to thirty children, one child probably has ADHD. Altogether, this represents approximately two million children in America.

SI-trained therapists use a neurophysiologic approach to behavior that applies to and can improve hyperactivity and attention problems. This is a non-invasive first step for many parents, including those who do not want their children to use medication. SI-trained therapists see hyperactive behavior as an information-processing problem in the child's nervous system. They apply the neurophysiologic explanatory model to treatment provided by occupational, physical, and speech therapists.[6] Therapists trained in SI usually use the testing batteries developed especially for these children by Dr. Ayres.[7]

In our experience, some children benefit from the addition of a medical intervention, possibly a year after SI therapy has been initiated. Other children who are referred for SI therapy are already taking a drug for hyperactivity at the time they begin therapy. We usually see positive changes in these children when therapy is added to a medication regimen. Frequently, the child's medicine can be lessened and eventually stopped.

A Brief History of SI Therapy

One of the first breakthroughs in the treatment of hyperactive children took place when Dr. A. J. Ayres saw the connection between tactile defensiveness and hyperactivity. The term *tactile defensiveness* was coined by Dr. Ayres to refer to a reaction to touch.[8] For example, one might experience an unexpected touch or being bumped unexpectedly as unpleasant or threatening, or one might be annoyed or react in a defensive fashion. The term *touch aversion* also refers to a negative experience of various tactile stimuli, but in this case, one experiences it as unpleasant and then actively avoids it. For example, one might react to the stimulus of clothing, textures, or even splashed water with either slight aggression or avoidance. We now make a distinction between the behaviors of aggression and avoidance. In each case, however, the negative energy with which one deals with a stimulus can be distracting and lead to distractibility and hyperactivity in general.

In the last decade, a scientific effort led by Dr. Lucy Jane Miller advocated for use of the name *sensory processing disorders* (SPD).[9] One of the major goals of this campaign was to have this diagnosis accepted in the *Diagnostic and Statistical Manual* (DSM-IV), the guidebook that sets standards for diagnosis by the medical community worldwide. Miller recently published a book entitled *Sensational Kids* that has "sensory processing disorders" in its subtitle. In this book, we use the term *sensory integration dysfunction.* However, the trend in future years will likely be to use *sensory processing disorders* instead.

How We Process Stimuli

Sensory information, or *stimuli,* is the information in our direct environment that is perceived through the senses. We receive stimuli from sounds, light, and movement through our muscles and joints. What we eat and drink gives us sensations, or stimuli. We are actually bombarded with all types of stimuli day and night, and our nervous systems must respond to these stimuli (Figure 1.1), relegate them to the background, or chose to ignore them.[10]

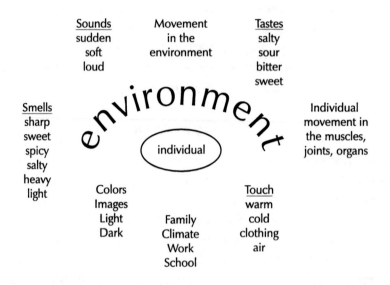

FIGURE 1.1. *We each exist and function in our own unique, personal environment. We are bombarded with stimuli. The nervous system filters the information and makes sure that we absorb and process the information we need to function.*

Not everyone reacts the same way to the same stimuli. What is important is *what* is reacted upon and *what* is not. The stimuli to which we react can be different for each individual. Each person has his or her own genetic make-up, which is responsible for that person's physical and psychological characteristics, which in turn shape the person's needs. For example, one person likes a darkened environment, while another person prefers a well-lit room. Some people concentrate better in a quiet environment and others concentrate better if music is playing. Within the extremes, all variations are possible.

From Stimuli to Reaction

Our neurological processes help us absorb, process, and react to the stimuli in our immediate environment (Figure 1.2). Information is received by the different senses and the central nervous system and is coordinated by the brain. The relevance of information and how it interacts with other information is defined in the brain. After organizing the information, the brain directs our body and our behavior. If the information is assembled properly within the brain, then our daily life tends to function smoothly. This helps establish the basis for good social skills.

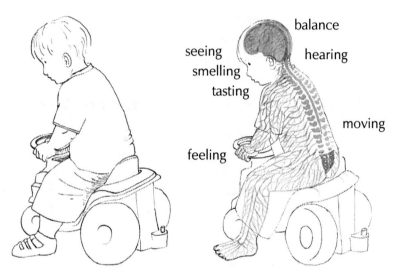

FIGURE 1.2. Neurological processes help us process stimuli.

Problems in Processing Stimuli

Sometimes children do not process stimuli well. Problems processing stimuli can manifest in various ways. Moreover, these ways of processing stimuli can vary from child to child. For example, one child might be very still while another might be very active, or one child might speak well and another might not. Or, problems processing stimuli might cause one child to move differently from the way other children move.

To get a sense of how this process works, imagine the nervous system as a tangle of electrical wires, interspersed with switches and connectors, and lit by lamps at the ends. In a calm child, only one of these lamps might light up for each stimulus. In a hyperactive child, the same stimulus might light up at least fifteen lamps. Because of this exaggerated reaction, the hyperactive child might not be able to analyze or organize his or her thoughts or keep them in balance. Inappropriate reactions to stimuli are called *sensory integration dysfunction,* or simply *SI problems.*

This book is about very active children. Some of these children are diagnosed with attention deficit hyperactivity disorder (ADHD) by doctors, psychologists, or psychiatrists upon examination. (ADHD is discussed in Chapter 2.) Outside of health-care circles, people in a child's environment sometimes offer informal diagnoses. Educators, for example, see and identify these children all the time, and their identification is based on the learning and social behaviors exhibited.[11] SI-trained therapists, on the other hand, are trained to identify the underlying neurophysiologic basis for the behavior and to help the child's central nervous system function in a better fashion.[12]

Environment: Where, with whom, and how do you live?

All children are part of the environments in which they live. The environment does not just refer to the parents, brothers and sisters, teachers, and other people with whom the child comes into contact. It also refers to how the child lives and to the kind of home in which he or she lives, sleeps, and plays. With what kind of toys does the child play? How much time is spent using the computer? Is he or she an only child or are there more children in the house?

Sensory Integration Diagnosis

When SI-trained therapists are invited to evaluate a child with problems, they have a battery of screenings, tests, and clinical observations from which to choose to help them make the decision about whether a child should have an intervention. Parents, caretakers, or teachers are the ones who frequently first identify the problem. In the next section we will discuss many of the behaviors that children with sensory-processing problems exhibit.

Dealing with Divergent Behavior

Adults generally have trouble dealing with a child who has problems processing stimuli and behaves in what adults consider to be a different way. They are definitely troubled by a child who is easily distracted, has no patience, is disorganized and impulsive, is always active, is very noisy, or in any other way disturbs adults in their daily activities. It can be difficult to understand that the child does not behave this way on purpose but is *simply unable* to behave in any other way.

If you understand this and learn to view your hyperactive child in a different way, you may notice that the child has a unique personality. It may also become apparent that your child has many positive characteristics, such as being friendly, spontaneous, always engaged and interesting, and always ready for an adventure. This perception can become the basis for dealing more effectively with your child's divergent behavior.

Seeking Help and Evaluation

Children are brought to an SI therapist because they are in need of help for functional problems in their life. The therapist first collects information related to how the child functions at home and at school, as well as any additional problems.

The therapist may use questions such as the following:

- Which sensory system works well? Which system requires attention? Which system dominates the other senses?

- Is there a problem in the processing of information or in the execution of directions?

- Why does the child behave in a particular way?

- Is the child sufficiently alert?

In addition, evaluation procedures include standardized tests that have been designed for children with these problems.[13] However, some children do not respond to standardized tests, and the therapist testing them has to rely on his or her power of observation to establish the goals for SI therapy.

SI Diagnosis

After conducting an extensive examination, the therapist uses the results of the tests and/or observations to help determine the treatment plan and direction SI therapy should take. The therapy can be designed accordingly to ensure that all sensory-system functions are addressed efficiently.

One possible SI diagnosis is that the child has a problem with the processing of tactile sensations. Psychologists or other professionals might give the child another diagnosis, such as ADHD. In fact, different diagnoses may be given to the same child by various professionals, even if the symptoms are identical. Occasionally, the child is only evaluated by an SI therapist, so the child only receives an SI diagnosis.

Teachers, parents, and non-SI-trained therapists usually give diagnoses that deal with the symptoms of the problem, while SI-trained therapists focus on the *cause* of the symptoms. For example, in the case of a child with ADHD, an SI therapist might focus the diagnosis on the child's poor processing of sensory information, which leads to impulsive behavior, distractibility, incessant movement, and inattention.[14]

Possible Causes of SI Problems

As parents search for the cause of the problems exhibited by their hyperactive child, they may wonder if a genetic factor is involved. Some may blame themselves for having poor parenting skills. Health-care givers, on the other hand, may seek a physical cause because they see the problem in the framework of medical prevention and treatment.

At this time, no one knows exactly why SI problems originate. Research points in several possible directions, most of which are physical:[15]

- Genetic factors
- Viruses, illnesses, alcohol or medicine use previous to or during pregnancy; extreme stress during pregnancy
- Premature birth
- Birth trauma (e.g., oxygen depletion, an emergency C-section) or an operation immediately following birth
- Circumstances after the birth (e.g., environmental pollution, too little or too much stimulation, staying in the hospital too long, emotional or physical neglect, attachment difficulties)

Dr. J. Kimball, in the process of investigating which children responded best to the medications Ritalin and Cylert, investigated two probable causes of hyperactivity due to differences in brain processing, especially relating to the vestibular system.[16] Using the Southern California Sensory Integration Tests and the Southern California Post Rotary Nystagmus Test, she found one group of children became very active in order to raise their arousal level (see

Chapter 3). This occurred through the brain stem, the portion of the brain that integrates many sensory channels. To raise their arousal, these children added more movement, activity, noise, or other stimulation. If they added the right amount of stimulation, integrated primarily through their brain stems, they would become calm and organized. These children tended to respond well to stimulant medications.

The second probable cause of hyperactivity Kimball investigated was in the group of children who had difficulties in dampening or inhibiting the amount of information processed in the cortex. When children with this problem were exposed to increased noise, movement, or other stimulation, they did not calm down, but rather became more excitable. These children were the children who did not respond well to the medications.

One Way to Understand a Child

Children (and adults) can be categorized into several types, based on their ability to integrate sensory information.[17] Such categorizations can help parents to better understand their hyperactive child, although they do not necessarily suggest a cause for the behavior. Some of these categories overlap, as well.

The Sensation-Seeking Type

The first type of child is not easily stimulated, yet wants stimulation and reacts actively to the stimuli received. This sensation-seeking type of child seeks strong stimuli. For example, these children love strong flavors, loud noises, and quick movements. They are prepared to improvise and enjoy activities in their environment. Thrill-seeking behavior is often seen in these children, especially when they are young, but is seen less often as they approach adulthood. Seeking new sensations is perfectly all right but is not appropriate in all situations. When these sensation-seekers have few stimuli, they are bored and become restless.

The Poor-Registration Type

The second type of child reacts calmly and in a passive manner when presented with stimuli. These children are in a state that is conducive to concentration, even when much is happening in their direct environment. To the outside world, these children might seem uninterested or somewhat withdrawn. They may appear unmotivated to communicate and may be described as registering very little information.

The Sensation-Avoiding Type

The third type of child is very attentive and observant of the environment and wants to be in control of the various stimuli in their environment. This is the avoidant type of child. Children in this category are easily stimulated and frequently overstimulated, and they seek to actively reduce stimuli to avoid this unpleasant stimulation. They structure their daily lives and make rules to attempt to do this; they love routines. In this way, they can consciously control incoming stimuli.

The Sensitive-to-Stimuli Type

The fourth type of child is quickly stimulated and reacts clearly to various stimuli. These children are constantly aware of their environment and are easily distracted. They may complain readily. They also may not sit still or work on a task because they are annoyed by some sound that other children hardly notice, and they may only be able to finish the task when the annoying stimuli (e.g., noises or certain sounds) are first eliminated. These children are the oversensitive type.

Types 1 and 4 are typical among hyperactive children. In Type 1 children, hyperactive behavior is caused by a lack of incoming stimuli. The child feels a need to search out more information. For example, the child wants to explore everything (touch), runs around (balance), wants to look through everything (sight), is very noisy (hearing), or wants to eat things that are strongly flavored (taste).

Type 4 children receive a great deal of stimuli but cannot filter it well. These children do not know how to manage the stimuli and thus become easily distracted. The child sees, hears, feels, and smells everything around, but cannot concentrate on the task at hand.

Case Study: Problems with the Sense of Touch

MANDY

Mandy was a healthy baby. When she was ten months old, she developed encephalomyelitis, an inflammation of the lining of the brain. Fortunately, she received antibiotics in time and recovered well. Everyone felt relieved. Mandy grew normally and was rarely sick, except for a few serious middle ear infections. Now that she is six years old, she enjoys going to school. She is an active child, enjoys playing sports, and has many friends.

However, Mandy is not always the easiest child. Those people who see her only occasionally do not notice that Mandy can be very annoying. Sometimes, when visitors come, she hides in her room. She never wants to be held. If someone tries to hold her, she makes a joke and pulls away. She hates being tickled and dislikes fighting or any kind of roughhousing. She is also very picky about clothing and will only wear cotton fabrics, preferably thin, tight T-shirts and jeans. She hates sweatpants and shirts. Woolen sweaters feel itchy to her, and a label touching her neck really irritates her. She prefers to sit in the back of the class and talk to her friends. From there, she can see the rest of the children.

Mandy is an example of a Type 4 child. She is always alert to irritants in her environment. She pays extra attention to any kind of perceived threat: her clothing, her classmates, the movement of other people. She has tried to lessen the effect of these annoying irritants. The price she pays is that she has less attention to give to other issues or activities, such as listening to her teacher. Instead of paying attention, she is busy attempting to control who sits next to her and what that person is doing. She might be able to concentrate on her studies a little better if she were not so distracted by how much her clothing irritates her. Interacting with her family might be more pleasant if she did not feel so threatened by hugs, kisses, or roughhousing.

Mandy is often distracted from the very activities in which she wants and needs to participate. This often happens to people who have ADHD. Fortunately, many find a way to reduce the effects of the irritating stimuli. Mandy's strategy includes participating in sports as frequently as possible, which allows her to remain in motion, exercise her muscles, and become more balanced. While playing sports, Mandy stimulates the proprioceptors, small sensors in the muscles that help people feel movement and postures. These sensors are also involved in deliberate efforts to diminish the effects of negative tactile stimuli. Sports such as weight lifting, gymnastics, judo, tai chi, qigong, wrestling, and horseback riding can balance an oversensitive tactile system. Many daily activities that use heavy muscle action provide this type of balance as well.

TIP Touching

Sports can help diminish oversensitivity to stimuli delivered through touch.

Questions about SI Therapy

SI therapy is discussed in great detail in Chapter 5, as well as throughout the book. The following questions are among those we hear most frequently, and so we have presented them here by way of introduction.

Q: Do hyperactive kids always need SI therapy?

A: No. Many children are very active, but not all are active because they have problems integrating sensory stimuli. Many children can be helped by treating them in a straightforward way and by offering them a clearly defined structure. Educational advice can also help. Social work can improve family dynamics. In addition, some parents choose to use a medication regimen for their children. A child may react so well to the medication that no other treatment is necessary.

Q: Which hyperactive children can be helped with SI therapy?

A: Children who can be helped include those who have behavioral problems, learning difficulties, or motor problems, and those whose parents find they do not function up to potential in school. Children who are unhappy, defiant, and quickly irritated are usually recommended for SI therapy because their problems are serious enough that their parents seek help.

Evaluation by an SI-trained therapist can determine whether a child is likely to benefit from SI therapy. Children for whom problems are identified in at least two different sensory systems will probably be helped by therapy. As a first step in the evaluation process, the therapist asks the child's parents and school personnel to fill out a questionnaire. You can find an example of this type of questionnaire in Chapter 8. Comparable checklists based on scientific research also are available.[18] Using these types of observational tools, the SI-trained therapist can decide if the results indicate a need for therapy. An expanded investigation follows, using standardized, normed tests in most instances.

Q: What is the procedure for getting a referral for SI therapy?

A: In many cases, children are referred to a SI-trained professional by a psychologist. Psychologist Robert Dunn, who practices near Amsterdam, in the Netherlands, told us he refers children if he sees a big difference between their verbal and performance capabilities, and if one symptom is hyperactivity. Another psychologist, C. Baltzley, who practices near Leiden, in the Netherlands, refers a child to a SI-trained therapist only if the child has motor problems as well as classic ADHD symptoms.

In the past, SI therapists received appropriate referrals when they contacted various professionals in their working area and explained the effects of therapy. Word of mouth, seeing results with specific children, and books such as this one have also led parents to actively seek SI therapy.

Q: If a child is recommended for SI therapy, isn't it enough to follow some tips at home?

A: Although books offer many handy tips for dealing with children who are hyperactive or who have ADHD, these tips cannot replace the developmental benefits derived from a long-term therapeutic intervention.

SI therapy can be given for several months or for a year or two. It can even require several years, depending on the intervention level at which a child begins. It is difficult to say how much time is needed because therapists work in different ways and each child and their family has unique needs. Children are usually treated during a 45-to-60-minute weekly session. Therapy ends when the pre-established goals have been realized. The younger the child is when therapy starts, the fewer sessions it usually takes.

Q: Which medical personnel include SI principles in their practice?

A: Occupational, physical, and speech therapists are all eligible to take postgraduate courses in SI therapy. These special SI courses are indispensable for studying neurology, diagnostics, and therapeutic interventions that can help children take the next step in their development. SI therapy can be used as an extra tool, alongside traditional therapeutic intervention. Some therapists who learn basic SI skills in an undergraduate course claim to be trained in SI therapy. However, their knowledge is usually not equivalent to that acquired through graduate or postgraduate coursework. There are exceptions, of course. Just remember that it is important to check the training background of a therapist before beginning therapy.

You may find that various types of professionals, all of whom have been trained in SI therapy, use different SI methods with the same child. For example, a speech therapist may focus on getting the child to breathe properly while he or she sits on a ball or swing set. A physiotherapist may use music therapy while a child does a jumping game that involves motor skills. An occupational therapist may use deep pressure techniques while a child sips lemonade or blows bubbles, in order to help that child learn how to improve eating skills. Countless examples could be cited.

Q: *What additional helpers or professionals might a child need?*

A: Effective therapy can lead to improved behavior, functioning, and emotional stability, as well as to an improved capacity to learn. Children who have more than one type of problem are often seen by more than one type of therapist. A child might, for example, receive speech therapy, occupational therapy, and physiotherapy to treat different problem areas (e.g., as described in the above question). Doctors, chiropractors, orthopedists, psychologists, psychiatrists, and special needs teachers may all work with the child during the same time period. A cooperative working relationship between all involved professionals is in the best interest of the child and the parents.

Chapter 2

The Hyperactive Child

A classroom is not the right place for acting wildly.

Active or Hyperactive?

You probably are reading this book because you have a very active child or you know one. All children can be very active occasionally or can make more than enough noise. However, some children attract notice because they are so difficult to control, exhibit overactive behavior, or talk all the time. It is difficult for these children to control their behavior, even though they can be very agreeable at times. They can be funny, full of energy, and well behaved when you deal with them one-on-one.

Dealing with these children is often a challenge, even though they can be charming, creative, and happy little people. When everything is going well, their refreshing point of view can make life exciting. However, when they have problems, they may camouflage them by playing "the clown," for example. Many children at school enjoy seeing these children play the clown or do deliberately silly things, and the teacher may even laugh at them, despite knowing this is not appropriate behavior. A child displaying this type of behavior temporarily avoids attending to academic material.

Two diagnostic categories are used for highly active children: attention deficit hyperactivity disorder (ADHD) and attention deficit disorder (ADD). These disorders, their relationship with SI, and factors that can cause hyperactivity are discussed in this chapter.

Attention Deficit Hyperactivity Disorder

Hyperactivity is the chief symptom of ADHD. This disorder is recognizable through its display of inattention and incessant movement (Figure 2.1). Children with ADHD have a problem with self-regulation and cannot organize behavior in a way that is appropriate to the situation.[1]

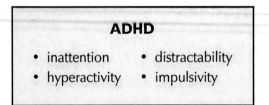

ADHD

- inattention
- hyperactivity
- distractability
- impulsivity

FIGURE 2.1. Characteristics of ADHD

ADHD has also been termed a *performance problem.*[2] Children who have ADHD cannot seem to find the right behavior to plan or finish a specific task in a set timeframe. ADHD as a continuing problem may be less evident in older children and adults because they may have learned to compensate for these shortcomings. Nevertheless, many of these individuals continue to have great difficulty in their jobs and home life due to ADHD.

Doctors, psychiatrists, and other health-care givers make the diagnosis of ADHD on the basis of observing a certain number of behaviors performed by the child or the adult. For some time it was thought that many doctors and psychiatrists in both America and the Netherlands were diagnosing many, many children—perhaps too many—as having ADHD and consequently prescribing Ritalin for them. To determine if this was the case, we evaluated the diagnoses of the children attending a public Amsterdam outpatient center between 2000 and 2006. This small group of 26 children had been evaluated by the full team. They were referred to an occupational therapist specializing in SI, as well as to other medical and family intervention practitioners. We evaluated the primary symptoms of the child and then compared the diagnoses. This led us to conclude that the percentage of children receiving a diagnosis of ADHD had actually declined in relationship to the percentage of other groups (e.g., children with conduct disorders, with problems dealing with divorce, or with problematic living conditions due to immigration, etc.). The reason for this is not clear, but we suspect it is related to the refinement of the diagnostic criteria, which emphasize other aspects of the child's life. So it appeared that the doctors in this clinic had become more selective with their primary diagnosis, frequently using the "ADHD/ADD" as a secondary diagnosis.

Attention Deficit Disorder

Attention deficit disorder (ADD) is a different diagnosis from ADHD. For children with ADD, the problem is inattention without hyperactivity. Such children are not hyperactive. The DSM-IV includes a precise description of the symptoms that must be present for such a diagnosis. As with ADHD, the goal is for all medical personnel to arrive at the same diagnosis.

Differences and Similarities Between ADHD and SI Problems

As you can see in Table 1 (on the next page), SI problems can overlap with ADHD symptoms, but the two also can be quite different. A child who has an SI disorder that appears to be "causing" ADHD will possibly present with different problems involving the sensory systems than will a child without ADHD symptoms. If SI problems are evident, this child should be given the chance for an SI intervention.

JOEY

Joey is a funny boy of seven who can be very active. He walks around most of the time, moves frequently, and talks constantly. Joey comes across as insecure and demands a great deal of attention from the adults in his life. He was born healthy after a normal pregnancy and delivery. Until now, Joey's motor skills have developed slowly. He did not start to walk until he was a year and a half. He did not dress or undress himself until he was five. He is not yet toilet trained at night and has trouble with swimming and with riding a two-wheel bike. He cannot open or close buttons or tie his shoelaces. He did not want to lie on his stomach when he was a baby. Joey did not play with others until an older than normal age. No relevant medical history explains this delay. Nine months ago, a swimming instructor, his doctor, and his parents recognized his problems for the first time. (Note: Of course, Joey had various problems during his life, but frequently parents think that that is "just the way he is." Families also tend to adapt their whole lifestyle to their child's behavior. Sometimes this is perfectly acceptable, but frequently the school situation

Table 1. Characteristics of ADHD and SI problems[3]

Characteristic	Problem	For ADHD child	For SI child
Level of Activity: amount of movement (e.g., during sleeping, eating, playing)	Level of activity is not appropriate to the situation	Restless, wriggling, or exaggerated movements; constantly runs around; messy	Quickly tires or is never tired; wound up or dull; looks for stimuli or tries to reduce stimulation; always wants to move or does not want to move
Rhythm: regularity in body functions (e.g., hunger, sleeping, elimination)	Rhythm diverges from what is considered appropriate to the age; a child's physical and sensory condition can influence rhythm	Eating or sleeping problems; being obstinate	Irregular sleep/wake cycles; obstinacy; delay in learning meaningful words
Approachability/ reserve: nature of the first reaction to new stimuli (e.g., new situations, people, places, food, toys, procedures)	Social problems are created in reaction to new stimuli	Anxious, bashful, shy	Avoiding eye contact; not noticing if other people come into room
Adaptability: ease with which someone can relate to new stimuli	Environment is dominated by the child's wishes	Always wants control over the situation, quickly overwrought by changes in the environment	Overwrought if something changes with personal hygiene rituals (e.g. washing hair, brushing teeth)
Intensity of reactions: amount of energy used irrespective of the situation	Child has no control over the energy expended in his or her reactions	Impulsive, wound up; slumped shoulders; moody; cries easily or without provocation; oversensitivity to criticism; quickly overstimulated	Emotional; aggressive reaction to sensory stimuli (e.g., light or touch); moody; frustrated when something does not work; self-directed anger and shyness

Table 1. Characteristics of ADHD and SI problems[3]

Characteristic	Problem	For ADHD child	For SI child
Humor: behavior that is pleasant and friendly or unpleasant and unfriendly	Child cannot always analyze a situation correctly (e.g., may feel threatened when no threat is present)	Sudden, drastic change of humor; moody	Exaggeratedly affectionate or attached; cannot express emotions; no sense of humor; exaggeratedly sensitive; exaggerated reactions
Follow-through potential: being able to complete one activity	The child cannot satisfy the demands of his or her environment	No matter what child is doing, he or she cannot stop an activity	Gives up quickly; difficult to motivate; attempts tasks in an illogical order and is angry if efforts do not work
Distractibility: effect of internal and external stimuli on what one is attempting to do	Child cannot concentrate on the job at hand	Tries to complete things quickly and still is distracted; cannot pay attention for long enough to complete tasks (e.g., at home, at school, or when playing)	Seems to shut down in a busy environment; seeks stimulation or is distracted by light, sound, or sudden touch
Stimuli threshold: amount of stimuli (e.g., light and sound) needed to provoke a reaction	Child's reaction to stimuli is disturbing to him or her and to everyone in the surroundings	Oversensitive to stimuli, even as a baby; reacts too much or too little to stimuli in the environment	Negative behavioral reactions to loud sounds (e.g., holds hands over ears); does not care for strong odors or continually notices them; sensitive to certain fabrics and materials; has a different perception of pain and temperature; reacts too little or too much to touch or movement; has a negative reaction to certain types of food (e.g., grainy, raw, fine, hard, soft)

cannot allow for that. Denial on the part of parents is frequently the first emotion when one's child is being diagnosed as having problems. This reaction is very natural and very common. But when parents have a situation or problems that can no longer be escaped, the family needs to arrive at a new constructive phase for their child. On the other hand, some parents have difficulty finding professionals who really see the child's problems and are able to identify their condition as Sensory Integration Dysfunction. So when Joey's parents came to the conclusion Joey's problem was SI based, it was time to find an appropriately trained therapist. Making this decision was a tremendous relief for them.)

At this point, Joey

- has difficulty concentrating when his surroundings are noisy, particularly when affected by unexpected sounds

- has difficulty carrying out orders, does not always seem to understand what someone is saying to him, and has trouble expressing himself

- enjoys making noise

- sometimes becomes anxious when he is on a swing, seesaw, or other playground equipment and has difficulty catching himself when he falls

- has difficulty with bright light

- is afraid of the dark

- has a lazy right eye

- finds it difficult to accept being touched or caressed and avoids being kissed (although problems with hair washing and nail trimming are usually seen in combination with touch issues, these are not a problem for Joey)

- avoids wearing certain clothes and eating certain types of food

- has problems riding a bike, is not even motivated to try, but is mad because all his friends can ride bikes

- sometimes appears to have less strength than other children have, does not seem to use both halves of his body in an appropriate fashion, and has difficulty sitting up straight

- has difficulty using the correct amount of strength for a task (e.g., sometimes squeezing something too hard and at other times misjudging how heavy an object is)

- has a generally clumsy movement pattern; does not seem fluid in his movements

- has fine motor problems (e.g., gets cramps holding a pen, has bad aim, finds exact tasks difficult)

- has a poorly developed image of his body; draws an incomplete image of a person, has difficulty with spatial relations

- has some difficulty playing alone, playing with other children, and listening to a story

- has little interest in playing outside

- has sloppy eating habits

- is afraid of new things, is quickly irritated, is moody, sometimes quickly tires, and often is aggressive without a discernible reason and hits anything within reach

- has problems with impulsivity, does things before he thinks

- displays enormous bravado (i.e., compensates by being very boastful) in class

- sometimes exhibits nervous behavior in school, has little self-esteem, is unable to sit still, has poor concentration, and is not consistent in school performance

In sum, Joey has tactile (touch), auditory (hearing), visual, and proprioceptive (muscles and joints) system problems. His most crucial problem is an aversion to touch—he never wants to be touched by others. Joey is not feeling comfortable with his body due to this and the other experiences he perceives as negative: wearing certain types of clothes and eating certain types of food. This sensory information may just be too much for him and may feel like it is bombarding him. He may be able to verbalize this. Most other children would be fine with this information, but for Joey, it probably is the cause of his inattention and hyperactivity as well as social problems, such as not wanting to play with others. He also may appear preoccupied because he is focusing—either consciously or unconsciously—on touch stimuli and how to avoid them. Joey's behavior comes across to others as insecure and frustrated because he cannot do what he wants to do.

Possible Factors that Could Cause Hyperactive Behavior

Hyperactive children are found in all kinds of families: rich and poor, large and small. There are many, many possible causes of hyperactivity. According to the research literature, not all of these causes are fully understood, and their relationship is ambiguous. Much like the conundrum of the chicken and the egg, it often is not clear whether a factor is the cause of hyperactive behavior or the result of it.

In this section we look at several possible causal factors. These include both external and internal factors. On the one hand, allergies and feelings of stress can be influenced by too much external stimulation and cause hyperactivity. On the other hand, the ability to self-regulate, remain balanced, stay organized, and behave appropriately can be influenced by the internal regulation of the central nervous system.

Problems Planning and Organizing

Motor planning refers to the ability to organize behaviors in order to accomplish something new. It includes planning a course of action and sequencing the actions. It is the process of choosing a strategy. The plan is based on a person's body image. Body image is the picture a person forms of his or her own body: where the head is, how it feels, how it moves, and so forth. Body image guides a person in how to use his or her own body.

To figure out how to use your motor skills, you need to have a good sense of your muscles and joints, especially your hands and fingers. In addition, you need a well-developed sense of balance, a realistic body image, and the ability to pay attention. If you are doing something for the first time, you need to think of a plan for what to do and how to do it. This is called *motor planning* and it requires attention. When you have learned a skill, you no longer need the same degree of attention and motor planning. It becomes automatic. Think about driving a car. It takes some effort at first and then it becomes automatic.

Consider this example of motor planning in a preschooler's play. Ariel wants to build a wall from blocks and huge cushions; that is her *idea*. She has to think about where she will put the blocks and in which place she will set the cushions; that is her *plan*. She has to make a plan of proposed motor activities; that is her *execution*.

Or take the example of Suzanne playing hopscotch for the first time. All her attention has to be devoted to the game; she cannot think about anything else. She cannot pay attention to two things at the same time. After playing hopscotch a few times, she achieves control over the required motor skills. She no longer has to pay attention to every movement and can talk to her friends while she plays.

Attention is critical when making a plan. However, an ADHD child may not have the degree of perseverance or attention necessary to accomplish an unfamiliar task, or he may get mixed up due to the planning problem, and distracted and frustrated due to the situation. When the child develops a concentration problem, a well-trained SI therapist is needed to analyze which came first: the child's poor attention or the planning problem.

The ability to plan and organize a task requires being quick and efficient. When a child with ADHD cannot do a task quickly and efficiently and must repeat it again, one might think that child is hyperactive. For example, Billy is trying to fold a sweater and he just cannot do it. He keeps trying, yet every time he fails. The amount of time he will devote to mastering this skill depends on his ability to persist.

When frustration sets in, a child tries to finish the chore even more quickly, and thus does it sloppily. This might seem like lack of attention or hyperactivity. Parents often refer to this behavior as "quick and sloppy." However, the "quick-and-sloppy" method becomes less stressful than continuing to try to accomplish a task for which that child does not have the ability. In this case, the child may have a motor planning problem rather than an attention or hyperactivity problem.

Not being able to plan physical activities can be a problem in itself. Sometimes physical problems are made worse by a problem with attention. A child with ADHD is unable to maintain the attention required to produce well-executed, detailed work.

Motor planning problems can also be based on other SI problems. For example, Julie wants to learn to tie her shoelaces. She cannot sit still because her sense of balance is poor and she keeps falling over. This makes it harder for her hands to manipulate the laces. Unfortunately, the sense of feeling in Julie's fingers is also not developed enough for her to be able to feel the laces. In addition, her finger muscles are not strong enough to hold the laces tightly. Julie needs great determination and attention to learn this task, but her motor planning and task execution are hindered.

Julie's problem tying her shoelaces could have many causes. It could be physical due to a poor sense of balance. It could be tactile due to a poor sense of feeling in her fingertips. It could be due to poor feedback (i.e., not getting the information directly and quickly to the brain after an action). In this example, information from the proprioceptors in the muscles, joints, and ligaments in her hands, and especially her fingers, is not being adequately processed.

Julie may be viewed as having ADD or ADHD because of her inattentiveness and restless movements. However, her problem is actually a motor or a motor planning problem. In either case, she is engaged in a frustrating task. Careful observation and analysis of the task and all of its contributing circumstances are important for creating a good treatment plan.

Allergies

Many children who have sensory problems processing stimuli have allergies. They can have allergies to food, material, pollen, grass, fur, or medications. An oversensitive child does not have the ability to reduce or stop his or her reactions to these stimuli. A child without these problems is more likely to be able to do so.[4] Usually, children are not bothered by dust in the house or pollen in the air. But a child who is oversensitive is both bothered and distracted by them.

An important function of the brain is to sort out which stimuli are not relevant and to set these aside. Choosing not to react to certain stimuli is the brain's way of helping a child focus on important stimuli, such as the teacher's voice. If the child can avoid being distracted by allergens, that child's ability to pay attention will improve; at least sneezing or watery eyes will not divert his or her attention.

One possible cause of hyperactivity and ADHD is the effect of food additives; this relationship has been the subject of research since the 1970s.[5] Certain food additives, such as dyes, are believed to cause hyperactivity. Recently, the relationship between food additives and hyperactivity has attracted renewed interest. One carefully executed study showed that the behavior of children with ADHD improved when they followed a restricted diet that limited them to certain types of foods.[6] This approach introduced foods slowly—step-by-step—until the best diet for each individual child was identified. While these results are impressive, the researchers concluded a long-term study was needed for verification. Since then, a pilot study with more than forty children with ADHD has reinforced the earlier findings.[7]

A strict diet can be taxing for children and their parents. If a child already feels set apart, a special diet may only serve to enhance that feeling.

Sleep Problems

A child who does not get enough sleep on a given night may be much more quickly irritated the next day and exhibit signs of hyperactivity and an inability to pay attention. Usually, the child will feel a need to move to stay awake and alert. This may give the impression of hyperactivity.

Sometimes a child has problems achieving a good sleep-waking cycle. This can happen for different reasons. Perhaps the child simply needs more sleep. Perhaps the child had difficulty falling asleep as a baby because he or she did not feel comfortable alone. Or the problem could be that the child was not able to find comfort by sucking his or her thumb. Perhaps the child did not like the sensation of thumb sucking, or the parents did not approve of this habit.

Another cause of sleep problems is separation anxiety, in which children find it hard to sleep in a bed without their parents. Other children are so busy during the day that they become too wound up to fall asleep at night. This is described as a high level of *arousal* (see Chapter 3).

Aside from not being able to fall asleep, children may have trouble staying asleep. Possible causes are oversensitivity to noises and tactile sensations. A child who does not feel comfortable in pajamas, is bothered by the sheets or blankets, or is oversensitive to temperature probably has an aversion response to touch.[8]

Eating Problems

Some children are fussy eaters. They may only want hot food or cold food. Or they may only want to eat soft, white food or a strange combination of foods. This diet suits their sensory processing. In addition to being difficult for parents and causing trouble at mealtimes, this eating behavior can result in nutritional deficiencies, which in turn affect the child's behavior and development. Sometimes these nutritional deficiencies can be the cause of hyperactive behavior.[9]

Environmental Problems

Exposure to too many stimuli in the environment can cause stress in a child's life. The noise level in the family home (e.g., television noise in the background, talking loudly to be heard over the noise of the television, loud music, and a large number of people talking at once) can all be stressful.

A quickly paced life and high expectations can create a feeling of stress in certain children. If children react with outbursts, irritation, whining, and hanging onto their parents, these behaviors can be interpreted as hyperactivity and attention problems. Parents need to consider such questions as the following: How much time does the child play outside? Are the child's muscles exercised properly? Does the child have a chance to expend his or her energy?

Various poisonous substances present in the environment can also cause problems. The effects of minimal toxin exposure during pregnancy and early childhood are not well known. However, research shows that lead poisoning and exposure to medications, recreational drugs, or alcohol in the womb can lead to ADHD symptoms.[10] Very large amounts of a poisonous material can result in problems that are more serious and complex than ADHD, such as fetal alcohol syndrome. Glue sniffing can also cause attention deficit problems.

Parents, Children, and Emotions

In previous generations, little therapeutic attention was given to hyperactive behavior. It has always been recognized as a behavioral problem, but families have had different reactions to their children's behaviors. If a child was too "hyper," people said that child was not raised properly. Threats, punishment, and even spankings made sure the child learned how to behave. Fortunately, times have changed and adults are now ready to see things from the child's perspective and to look for an underlying cause if children cannot behave themselves.

Understanding the Child

It is important to realize that negative behavior can be associated with an inability to process stimuli. This inability can make a child irritable. As a parent, it is hard to remain kind and patient if your child is being uncooperative, difficult, mean, or angry. In these situations, parents often want to explain to the child that he or she should not feel so angry, mean, or display whatever other emotion they are experiencing. They may also try to reason with the child.

You will find it easier to get along with your hyperactive child if you can understand that the behavior is caused by a neurological problem (i.e., not being able to process stimuli) and that your child is not behaving this way on purpose.

Understanding for Parents and Caregivers

The strong emotions expressed by a hyperactive child can affect parents and caregivers emotionally. Because such a strong bond exists between the child and those who care for him or her, feelings can become quite intense. Feelings of anger, shame, sadness, and anxiety about the future can arise in those around the child. Parents also can feel hurt when other people look at their child disapprovingly. When this happens, it can be difficult to hear—and often impossible to follow—well-meaning advice from outsiders.

Reacting to a Hyperactive Child

Emotional

If you are feeling emotional in a negative way, it is not the right time to talk to your child about his or her behavior. It is a better idea to tell your child that you feel angry, sad, or afraid and that you need some time to regain your composure. You can say you will speak to your child in a few minutes, but be sure to do so.[11]

This way, the child understands that everyone has emotions. The child learns that adults can have strong emotions, but that adults can control their emotions. If children try to model this behavior, they can acquire self-confidence and eventually also achieve such control.

Calm

Your child may feel frustrated and inadequate. The following strategies can be useful if your child is in an irritable or emotional state:[12]

- Realize your child has a neurological problem.
- Understanding your child's limited capabilities can give you an opportunity to practice different strategies as suggested here.

- Recognize that you are in a crisis situation.
- Prevent the crisis by taking your child out of a frenetic environment.
- Stay calm.
- Reduce the amount of stimulation to which your child is exposed.
- Use stimuli that will calm your child, such as hugging or rocking (see Chapter 4 for more ideas).
- Make sure your child's life is structured.

Discipline

All children need discipline. They have to be able to understand and remember the rules. A hyperactive child needs structure that is tailored to his or her individual nervous system and takes into account the child's special needs in processing stimuli. A professional with SI training can help you institute a disciplinary plan. The following are some strategies that might be included in such a plan:

- Remember that discipline is only effective if it helps the child's brain to organize.
- Think twice before you say no. It is important to stay consistent.
- Rewarding good behavior and taking away privileges (e.g., watching television) because of bad behavior are the basic principles of discipline.
- A "grandmother's" rule of discipline is to work first and then play. However, a hyperactive child may need special activities (e.g., a movement break or drink break) between task intervals to help get the "work" accomplished.
- Keep your expectations reasonable and not higher than the child can handle. Remember that what is simple for someone else's child may be very difficult for your child.
- Remember to comment on and reinforce the good things your child does. Be positive. In this way, good behavior is stimulated. There is a good chance your child will remember this good behavior. Allowing your child to feel supported and accepted gives that child a stronger self-esteem basis for the rest of his or her life.

Questions about the Hyperactive Child

Q: How can I know what type of special activities might be of benefit to my child?

A: Children show us the activities they need to "soothe" their central nervous system or to pep it up so they can function at their best. Watch what your child does. For example, after school, does your child immediately go to the swing in the backyard for ten minutes? This might be what your child needs to become re-energized after a long bus ride or a trying afternoon. If you notice that this is what your child needs, you can suggest swinging on other occasions when you think your child needs it but does not go to the swing on his or her own. Of course, an indoor activity may be most appropriate. Perhaps your child would find a snuggle corner with a drink and a straw to be soothing. If a more energizing activity is needed, choose something physical you can do indoors, such as jumping on cushions (or the bed). Remember to supervise your child if the activity could be dangerous.

The activities provided for a child throughout the day have been called a "sensory diet."[13] This allows for a range of different activities that nourish the child's various needs. A trained SI therapist can help by offering a full battery of ideas.

Q: How can I determine if my child has food allergies?

A: You may already have observed a relationship between your child's behaviors and the food he or she eats just prior to engaging in those behaviors. For example, one mother told me that every time her child ate a hamburger with ketchup, she noticed he was hyperactive for the next few hours. She began to observe that the same effect occurred after he ate spaghetti with tomato sauce. So she eliminated tomato products from his diet.

Sometimes detecting an allergy can be as simple as making these kinds of observations. In other cases, closer attention might be required to identify patterns of reaction to various foods. Try writing down everything your child eats for a week and simultaneously noting any behavioral changes. If need be, this information can be given to a dietician, who will then draw professional conclusion and determine a course of action.

Q: I find it so difficult to discipline my child. Any tips?

A: If you have the attitude "I will just give my child what he or she wants" or

"I will let my child do what he or she wants *this time*," your child will not benefit from it. The message you are really communicating is "I am a loving caretaker, but I just don't have the energy at this moment to do what I know needs to be done."

We all have these kinds of moments. When these moments occur, give yourself the breaks you need so you have enough energy when it comes time to provide discipline for your child. This can mean taking as little as two minutes away from your family, without interruptions, a few times a day, to refresh yourself. You can also plan time for yourself on a weekly basis.

Your child needs to have a clear idea of what is expected. At the same time, rules occasionally have to be adjusted to fit the situation. This is especially the case when a child is not feeling well. For example, you may have a rule that your child has to put on his or her socks. However, on a day when your child is not feeling well, you may change the rule. You might say, "I'll put your socks over your toes and pull them over your heels because you aren't feeling well. But you can do the rest." In this way, you continue to provide discipline for your child, but you temper it with flexibility.

You can also consult your SI therapist for ideas that will help your with your child's special needs. The therapist can also offer referrals to other professionals in your neighborhood, if need be.

Chapter 3

What You Should Know about How the Brain Works

The brain is like a tangle of nerve connections.

===== **PETER** =====

Eight-year-old Peter is a very naïve, sweet, and open child. However, he can be extremely hyperactive, often out of control, very impatient, undisciplined, and sometimes aggressive. Yet, in a matter of seconds, he can revert to being his charming self. The switch can be so abrupt that it seems he must be handled with velvet gloves.

Our senses are bombarded with stimuli: noises, images, tactile sensations, movement, smells, and tastes. These stimuli are all detected by the brain. The brain receives approximately seven times more information than it can actually use. For this reason, it is important for the brain to filter information and to store information so it can be used when it is needed. Peter's brain is not efficient at selecting which stimuli to save. He reacts strongly to all the stimuli in his environment.

In this chapter, we discuss the relationship between a child's behavior and how the brain and sensory systems function. This may seem obvious, but other schools of therapy for ADHD approach the child quite differently. For example, some may use a motivational model for behavioral change. From our point of view, the most important functions of the brain are arousal (attention), registration, modulation, processing and interpreting, and reacting.

Arousal

Arousal is the state of the nervous system that pertains to how alert we are and whether it is possible for us to focus on carrying out specific tasks. Our level of arousal determines our ability to take in more stimuli at any given moment. Every twenty-four-hour time span includes a period of being awake and a period of sleeping. When we are awake, we are receptive to stimuli; for example, a child who is awake is receptive to his or her school lessons.

When we are awake, we are ready to receive new information and can listen attentively, eat heartily, recognize images, and have a sense of how we move. When we sleep, we are hardly conscious of stimuli. When we wake up, we often do not remember any more than that we have had a good night's sleep. This day-and-night rhythm has four different levels of arousal. Arousal is categorized by activity (Figure 3.1).

> **Example:** A hyperactive child who sleeps poorly is reacting to certain stimuli in his or her environment even while asleep. For example, the child may wake up if someone turns on a light. This is a disturbed reaction that should not occur during this period when a child's level of arousal is limited. The child should be able to sleep through a small noise or minor changes that take place in the room.

The level of arousal you find yourself in during sleep is shown in the left-hand column of Figure 3.1.

Deep Sleep

When we are sleeping, we need a greater number of stimuli to provoke attention. This is a normal situation.

> **Example:** Some hyperactive children find it difficult to wake up. A person who awakens such a child will find an unhappy, grouchy, ill-humored child. During the initial phase of waking up, this child is unable to deal with new stimuli or with any demands he or she may face, such as getting out of bed and dressing.

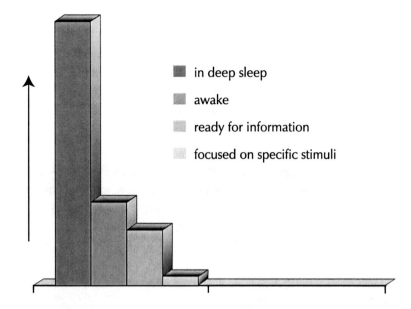

FIGURE 3.1. The amount of stimulation required for arousal depends on your state of consciousness at that moment.

Awake

When we are half awake, we find ourselves in an orientation phase: We can pay attention to a specific task only by acting in an automatic way. We need fewer stimuli to provoke attention than we do in the sleep state. We react more quickly and more directly to certain stimuli, such as hearing our name spoken. However, it is not yet possible to marshal enough attention for difficult or new things. Think of a moment when you are resting or have just woken up: What is happening around you seems to pass right by you, and you only register stimuli you consider really important.

Example: In a high state of arousal, a hyperactive child will react to almost every stimulus in and around the classroom. A little noise in the class or even the singing of a bird outside seems just as important to the child as does the voice of the teacher. The child is taking in all the information, but cannot select what is most important. Everything seems equally important.

Ready for Information

We are considered completely awake if our level of arousal enables us to receive appropriate information. Attention is directed to specific information, such as sounds, while other incoming stimuli are placed on the "back burner." Thus, when children in this state of arousal are in the classroom, they can follow the teacher's voice and still see what other children are doing.

> **Example:** A hyperactive child is not able to read a book or follow a conversation while riding in a crowded subway. This environment has many more stimuli than does a classroom. The child can pay attention to some stimuli, such as the person sitting next to him or her, but cannot absorb more specific information, such as the words on the page he is reading.

Focused on Specific Stimuli

On the fourth level of arousal, we have the greatest degree of concentration and give our direct attention to a specific person or problem. On this level, we can become even more selective about the information we absorb. We may notice other stimuli in the environment, but to a lesser degree, and we pay less attention to them. We direct our attention to whatever we want to absorb; thus, for example, we are able to read a book in a crowded bus.

For some people, however, this state of arousal may still be too low to be able to read a book in a crowded subway. A child with a problem reaching this state can be rocked to sleep by the movement of the train because he or she cannot maintain the level of focus associated with being awake and reading a book. This is similar to what happens to many children who have to sit still for a long time in class. They lose focus and cannot absorb further information.

> **TIP** **Paying Attention**
>
> If children sit still too long, they are not in a state in which it is easy to continue to focus. The child either becomes hyperactive or perhaps falls asleep. Pushing the child's hands together can bring him or her back to focusing on the lesson. It also helps to let the child stand for a minute, stamp his or her feet or even walk around, eat something (preferably a sour food), or take a short break. These strategies can help children return to a state of focus in which they can best absorb information.

Registration

A mother told us, "The environment in which Pete finds himself influences him greatly. If he is in a very busy environment, he does not seem to have any boundaries or brakes on his behavior. This is really a problem for both him and me."

When we receive information, it must be registered as meaningful. For example, if we are in danger of losing our balance, our brain registers that we are out of balance. How much information is absorbed concerning this situation depends on how focused we are at that moment. The information has to arrive at the right place in the brain to be recognized as meaningful. In the brain, complicated systems of nerve cells work to forward information to facilitate (help or strengthen) or to inhibit (block or reduce) the flow of information until it reaches the right destination. Pete, in the previous example, is not registering or absorbing information from his environment quickly and efficiently. His ability to register important stimuli is inadequate. He is easily distracted by unimportant stimuli, and he reacts to all the stimuli his brain has not filtered well.

The various senses can positively influence or support each other. In doing so, they can strengthen the perceived stimuli, and the stimuli can also be inhibited or reduced when another sensory system becomes involved. Both processes are necessary.

TIP Reading Aloud

Information received through one sense can influence information received from another sensory system. For this reason, most schools teach children to read by reading aloud to them. Sometimes you can also learn better if music is playing. Hearing then helps you process the words you read with your eyes.

Modulation

"Roy was very afraid of being touched and used his incessant activity to keep others away from him," Roy's mother reported.

Modulation is a regulatory function of the brain that ensures we receive exactly as many stimuli as needed in any given moment to pursue a balanced   ▦ **37** existence. Not too many, not too few, not too hard, and not too soft—we require the right balance so everything that needs to be done can be accomplished. In this way, modulation helps us achieve our goals. For example, if Roy can modulate the uneasy feelings he has about someone touching him, he can become calm enough and receptive enough to read a book. Sitting on a cushion or in someone's lap are other actions that might modulate the feeling of anxiety Roy has about being touched.

It is essential that incoming information be optimally received by a properly functioning nervous system and senses. When all involved systems cooperate efficiently, the right amount of modulation takes place and normal processing of information is possible. The brain knows which combination of stimuli we need to maintain our basic level of focus (Figure 3.2). Only after this level has been achieved can we choose an appropriate reaction.

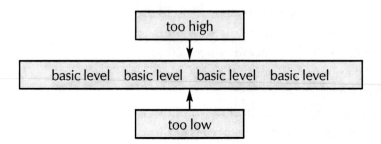

FIGURE 3.2. *The arrows show how the brain brings a plane of focus back into balance.*

Examples of modulation problems include:[1]

- Oversensitivity to movement (e.g., feeling carsick or becoming anxious about movement)
- Fear of heights (e.g., not daring to lift one's feet from the ground)
- Oversensitivity to sudden touch
- Oversensitivity to certain materials
- Oversensitivity to noise

Processing Information

JOEY

Joey is six years old and has a language problem. His hearing is normal, but he has trouble using letters, words, and sentences. He uses gestures to convey that he is trying to locate the right sounds in his mind. His movements are clumsy, as if he cannot coordinate his muscles.

Joey has difficulty processing language. Before Joey can attend to a language-related task, he needs to have the appropriate readiness or alertness to take in information and process it. He requires a great deal of time to search for a word. This is frequently referred to as a problem with the *retrieval process.*

Joey may not really be ready or at the best level for doing a language assignment. Getting him to the optimal level might be an important first step in his processing. Let us say his task is to say the word *roof* when he is shown a picture of a roof. He has the visual stimulus and must find in his cerebral cortex the matching sound. He knows that he is seeing a picture of a roof and he searches mentally for the combination of sounds that belong to that word. Thus, the process involves comparing the auditory word with the visual clue, the picture. Once he has the clue, he must retrieve the sequence of movements to pronounce the letters *r-o-o-f.*

Then he can say it. To improve his language ability, Joey has learned to repeat new words and sentences frequently. This stimulates the nerve cells to make better connections between these related areas.

A speech therapist who uses SI methods can do something extra for Joey during his therapy. She knows that Joey's brain works best when he is ready to process information and is optimally alert. She can offer him a swing or a bouncy ball to sit on so his brain is alert for incoming information. The area in the brain that processes movement is located very close to the areas that process sound.

The speech therapist also provides Joey with ways to access the information through other senses: hearing the word *roof,* seeing a picture of a roof, putting his hands on a roof. Thus, by combining movement and other senses, speech therapy helps Joey attain the optimal arousal level for learning and more quickly process the sensory information necessary for the use of language.

Reacting

LINDA

Linda has difficulty sitting up for long periods of time. Her balance is weak and her arms and legs are poorly coordinated. She inhales frequently as she speaks, especially when she is agitated. Yet she can easily focus and her fine motor skills are well developed.

After the brain processes and interprets information, there is usually a reaction. The reaction does not have to be made consciously. At the moment we are in danger of falling, the brain receives information from the eyes, the skin, the muscles, the joints, and the center of balance that lets it know the position of our body has suddenly changed. On the basis of this information, the brain plots a reaction. The proper reaction is to tense the muscles that ensure we remain standing. Or, if our reactions are a little slower, we may not be able to make that adjustment in time to prevent a fall or an injury. The brain can also decide not to react to incoming information. Not reacting can also be seen as a reaction. How we react to what our senses perceive determines ultimately how we react to our environment; this reaction is called *behavior.*

Problems exist if we react too strongly to mild stimuli; for example, if we become angry just because another person has accidentally bumped into us. Children with sensory processing problems often exhibit inappropriate reactions. Problems can also exist if we do not react strongly enough to stimuli; for example, if we belatedly notice we have stepped on something sharp. In this case, our late reaction can lead to greater injury to our foot.

Just as we have a specific reaction to sharp pain, we also have appropriate reactions to other, more general situations. For example, if we are at the movies, we sit quietly in our seats. All the parts of our central nervous system must work together to produce appropriate reactions. Often when people think about what it means to "behave appropriately," they think in terms of having conscious control over a given situation. But in the case of the hyperactive child, the central nervous system must function properly before that child can develop appropriate behaviors This behavior may be something the child understands and really wants to do but just cannot do, due to the way his nervous system is functioning at that moment.

Fight, Flight, Fright, and Freeze (FFFF)

If we cannot reduce stimuli, we can defend ourselves by fighting or fleeing, by becoming afraid, or by stiffening up. These are called *fight, flight, fright, and freeze* reactions (Figure 3.3). They are primitive reactions initiated by the nervous system designed to protect us from danger. Think, for example, of staying very still—freezing—when you smell smoke, and then fleeing.

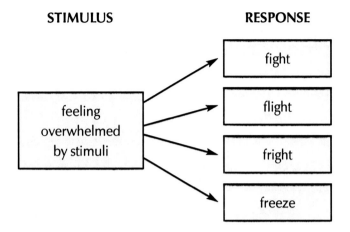

STIMULUS   **RESPONSE**

FIGURE 3.3. Children or adults who have a defensive reaction to sound or touch, for example, unconsciously choose between four primitive reactions when stimulated.

If we use these reactions unconsciously to react to stimuli that are not life threatening, they can distract us from engaging in activities such as reading or listening to a story or to music. Compared with other individuals, children and adults with ADHD are more easily stimulated into a fight, fright, flight, or freeze reaction and are more likely to remain in that state for a longer period of time.[2]

Planning Activities

When it is time to try something new, planning that activity requires the ability to focus. When we make a plan, we must determine exactly what will be done and how it will be done. To coordinate the plan, a complicated process takes place in the brain. Information is retrieved from the memory and compared with the plan being made. An important part of the plan is to efficiently determine the order of the steps: "First this, then that, then that, and only after these things are done will I carry out the plan and finish it." This planning has to take place very quickly.

To be able to do this, we need to have built up a good working memory that contains relevant information. The brain must have a few sample plans to consult; for example, a plan of what things will look like, a map of associated sounds, a map of associated sensations, a plan of how a certain posture or movement might be executed, a map of related smells.

Let's say Paul wants to study a new piece of music on the piano.

- Paul first decides if the piece of music is too difficult for him.

- He uses his eyes to scan the notes on the page and tries to form a picture of how they might sound. Paul couples what he sees with his memory of the sounds that belong to the notes.

- Little by little, he exercises his fingers on the keys, as he learned to do when reading music.

- He rehearses the piece thoroughly and repeats it many times.

- When Paul can play the piece in a technically complete fashion, he finishes by playing it with feeling.

Planning is required for every note he needs to play. Eventually, however, he knows the piece so well that he does not need to plan his finger action. His playing becomes so automatic it can be done as if he is using an "automatic pilot."

Questions

Q: My 10-year-old son is a regional champion tennis player, but his handwriting is messy and slow. And he is always forgetting to turn in his completed homework assignments at school the next day. Why is he so good at one thing and not at the others?

A: His ability to play tennis is performed on a different sensory motor circuitry than the circuitry needed to write letters and make words. For any ball sport, including tennis, football, soccer, badminton, etc., a person has to "keep his eye on the ball" in order to connect with either his racket or foot at the exact moment. Hitting a tennis ball well means that he has to place his body in the right position, running to the exact spot to hit the ball. He will need good overall power and even a certain amount of fine manipulation if he wants to aim the ball to go to a certain place.

As complicated as doing this sounds, it is not as complex as writing. First, writing is considered a fine motor activity that almost always develops after gross motor skills have developed. Hand dominance is necessary so that one hand can develop the ability to perform fine movements. Think about all the quick and precise fine movements that have to be made sequentially to just write the word "cat." By my count, the child has to make eight separate small movements. Our tennis star does not have his fine motor abilities at a level where he can do these small movements quickly and efficiently, which we call being able to write on "automatic pilot." He has to think of how every part of each letter goes. This is very energy consuming and takes him longer than other children.

Why can't he turn in homework papers the next day? Of course, this is something that is not really a pure motor task. It is an important activity that has several steps. Where does the homework go when it is completed at home? The next day, at the moment it needs to be turned in, is our child remembering that this is necessary? Maybe if he sees other children giving the teacher a paper, it will help his memory. Then the next step is figuring out where he put it. His own visual memory needs to help at this moment. He may remember that it is in his full book bag, but he may forget where in his book bag he put it. (Note that there are compensation techniques to help children with organization. Even singing little songs about tasks can be helpful (e.g., singing "I put my math in my green folder," etc.). Doing this allows the auditory system to help the visual memory.

Q: *Even though I can see my child is really tired, she is so busy at night that I cannot get her to sleep. Why is this?*

A: Children who have problems regulating their daily rhythms in general are frequently overstimulated at night and have difficulties feeling or figuring out how to get to that just-right level of inner quietness needed for sleep. This type of child tries to give herself extra stimuli to keep going. It helps her achieve her goal, staying up, but this is not what the child needs. Sleep is essential. As a parent, you can help change the level of stimulation at the end of the day.

Of course, most parents have a ritual before bedtime. Television and exciting games are usually too arousing. Reading is better. If your child has a room that can be made dark, this may help (a night light is certainly optional).

Once the child is in bed, a short back massage of no longer than three minutes can be helpful. The child knows there is no talking. The parent breathes deeply and slowly so the child can hear this and hopefully mimic it. The child is on his tummy and the parent, using a full, flat hand, begins the massage at the base of the head, the neck, and moves down to the end of the spine. The massage is done with medium-firm pressure. The full action of the massage movement from top to bottom should be very, very slow—it should last for a count of 5 to 6 seconds. Doing it even more slowly can be therapeutic. Before one hand leaves the base of the spine, the other hand is on the neck ready to start. In this way, the parent has one hand on the child at all times. At the end of 3 minutes, the parent places the full length of the forearm on the child's back for 1 to 2 seconds indicating that the massage is over. The parent and child should then say a quick "goodnight," and the child should not talk or get out of bed.[3]

Q: My child's teacher reports that he is distracted in school, but I when I see him playing with his Legos, he is very focused. Why can't he pay better attention at school?

A: The environment at school is, of course, different from that in your home. Usually there are less people in a household than in a classroom location, so he has less visual stimuli or people to see and possibly less noise and chatter. Some children need quiet in order to concentrate. Other children need music on in the background, which helps them in the process of attending and focusing.

Many children enjoy Legos. They are very simple, and that is why they are so popular. Just push one block into another. Some children want to follow the picture patterns to build a model. This does take more sensory skills. Building is a planning activity, and if a child is weak in this, he frequently needs to screen out all other stimuli in order to attend to this task only. It is, in fact, a good strategy for the child, but it has its drawbacks. This child becomes so focused, some say even "hyper-focused," that he cannot attend to anything else, like his mother calling him. So in general we want our children to be able to do more than one activity, like eating and listening to dinner conversation or dressing and telling a story.

Q: Why can't my child, George, do two things at once? I have noticed he needs to stop what he is doing in order to be able to attend to me.

A: In the example right above this one, we mentioned how children sometimes use this strategy of tuning out other stimuli in order to focus in on motor tasks. George might also need to focus on only a listening task. If you notice that your child needs to attend to only one thing, arrange things so that, in fact, only one item needs to be attended to at a time. Research has shown that the adult brain needs a short amount of time, 1 second, before another task can be attended to as well. Then both can continue. If an additional task is added in less than a second, this causes a jam up of information, but when given a full second, adults can do what we call multitasking.

When talking to your child who needs more time for language processing, remember that short, clear sentences are best. Some children benefit from looking at your mouth and watching your expressions, so always face your child. This combines auditory and visual stimuli to help your child. A language therapist might have additional ideas.

Q: *Why does my daughter appear to be in "dreamland," needing to be told things 2 or 3 times before she appears to understand what I have said to her? It seems to take her a while to react.*

A: This kind of child may not be registering the information that you are sending her way. The first step in understanding and acting on a command is being able to orient, or zero in on, what the stimulus is. In this case, the mother's request is not even attended to for several seconds. This is frustrating, but a possible explanation is that the child just does not have the right level of arousal to pick up the clues. Think of them as a child being woken up. If you told them at the moment of waking that they could do their favorite thing, like go to the zoo, they would be so sleepy or in such low arousal state that they might not even be looking at the person, much less taking in or even understanding what is being said to them.

With these children, the first step involves helping them to pep up. Pep-up activities like the trampoline, falling into cushions, hopping, blowing games, etc., are ways to wake up the child's central nervous system. When children are alert, they can better process higher-level tasks such as following directions.

Chapter 4

Understanding the Main Sensory Systems

Stimuli reach a child through the senses.

MANY PARENTS, TEACHERS, and caretakers feel it is important to know how their child's development compares with that of other children in the same age range. They may want to know if the child's development exceeds that of his or her peers. Equally important to many parents is whether their child is following the normal line of development or falling behind.

A well-known, often-used method of measuring development involves specific age-appropriate milestones. Examples include a baby's first laugh, which usually takes place at around six weeks, and a child's first steps, which are usually taken by 18 months. A child's development can be determined by looking at these milestones. Another way to look at the functioning of the child is to observe if the ability exists to process environmental stimuli normally. To be able to determine this, the normal ability at a certain age must be known.

All the senses are present when a baby is born. The newborn baby can feel, hear, see, smell, and taste; the sense of balance works; and the muscles and joints can perceive the way positions and movement feel. However, the baby still has to learn to use the senses. The nervous system has to develop so the whole sensory system works together. Specific tasks are delegated to different parts, and connections that coordinate input and keep a person in balance are established. This learning process is called the *development* of the senses (Figure 4.1).

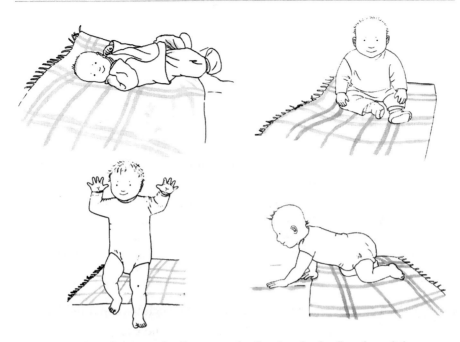

FIGURE 4.1. Developmental milestones: the first laugh; the first time sitting up, crawling, and walking.

This chapter describes the normal development of the senses. Because this book is intended to provide insight into possible deviations in development that your child may experience related to one or more sensory system, we suggest you read the entire chapter. In this way, you will be able to better understand the development of your child's sensory systems and have an easier time understanding the behavior of your child.

The Vestibular System:
The Sense of Balance and Orientation

Our vestibular system is frequently called the *balance* system, or in scientific circles the *equilibrium* system. These terms are somewhat limiting because the vestibular system involves so much more than balance and has an enormous effect on our lives.

The balance canals are found in the inner ear and constitute the vestibular system (Figure 4.2 on the next page).

Thanks to the vestibular system, our bodies can adjust during a physical change, such as shifting our balance forward, backward, to the side, up, or

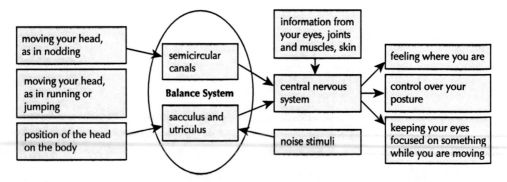

FIGURE 4.2. *Every movement the head makes is noted by the vestibular system. Information about these movements, as well as information received from other senses, is sent to the central nervous system. When the brain combines all this information, it can understand exactly where the body is, what its position should be at any given moment, and which eye movements are appropriate.*

down. If the system works well, we feel strong and solid; we may not fall very frequently, but if we do fall, we can recover quickly and well.

The vestibular system can be viewed as having five different parts:[1]

- A *motor* center to make three-dimensional movements

- An *emotional* center for self-regulation

- A *perceptual* center so we do not feel lost in space

- A *space/time* center in which the objects, people, and events we encounter can be combined

- An *orientation* center for integrating audio and visual stimuli in time and space with vestibular information

The basic balance system in the inner ear helps us keep our balance and deal with gravity. The result is the sense of equilibrium that is essential for us to feel safe in our bodies. Through the cooperative direction of our eyes and ears, we receive information about depth and distance. Our eyes and ears help us place ourselves in the environment; for example, they warn us about oncoming traffic.

The Importance of the Vestibular System

The vestibular system answers three of life's most important questions:

1. Where is up?

2. Where is down?

3. Where am I?

Other senses are also used to answer these questions.

1. If you want to know where "up" is, you feel gravity unconsciously and possibly tilt your head up to take a look. This also activates the sensory cells in the muscles and joints and stimulates the eyes. In a well-functioning vestibular system, the head and eye movements are well aligned.

2. When moving, every time you take a step, your body has to adapt to a new position. This demands finely tuned cooperation between the balance system, the eyes, and the sensory cells in the muscles and joints.

If you want to know where you are, you need a reference point that is stable. Therefore, movement has to be combined with standing still. To do this, stability is needed in the joints first. Sensory cells in the vestibular system provide the information to make this possible and answer the question, "Am I standing still?" The vestibular cells send information about gravity to the brain, which integrates this information with the information from the muscles and joints. The right tension in the muscles has to be built up so you are able to stand still enough to orient yourself. Your head must be stabilized by a strong neck. Using your eyes and ears, and your bodily sensations, you can determine exactly where you are (Figure 4.3)

FIGURE 4.3. The vestibular system = equilibrium = the balance system

The Normal Development of the Vestibular System

In the womb, the undeveloped fetus moves with the mother and adjusts itself until his or her head becomes locked into position at the end of the pregnancy. Immediately after birth, the baby cannot move much.

You can calm a restless baby with a rocking or swinging movement or with a steady vibration, such as taking the baby for a ride in a car. When the baby is picked up, the eyes move and the head tries to adapt itself to the movement.

TIP **Calming**

When your baby is resting in your arms, you can employ different vestibular stimuli. For example, you can use your body in a steady, slow swinging movement (Figure 4.4). Eventually, you can combine this movement with a rapid, yet smooth, rolling movement of your lower arm. Find the movement that is most calming for your baby. Every child is unique.

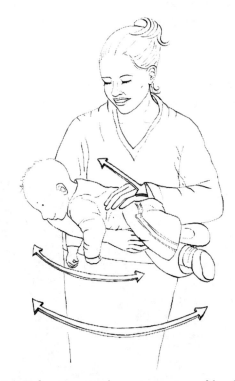

FIGURE 4.4. Calm, even motions are most soothing for a child.

When a baby is three to six months old, he or she has enough bodily control to roll over and begins to feel the sensation of turning. The baby lifts his or her head up when lying stomach down. Between six and eighteen months, the baby learns to hold his or her head high, to sit, to crawl, to stand, and to walk. The child learns to master gravity.

TIP Toddler

When learning to walk, your child needs to make repeated tries. Getting up, falling down, and using the muscles to provide strength and balance are very important for developing good motor skills. Give your child the room to learn, but take safety precautions. A room filled with large toys and a soft floor is the ideal place to master motor skills.

Between eighteen months and three years, your child's movements increase in speed; he or she learns to feel the sensation of speed. Your child derives pleasure from climbing and moving; is better at using his or her arms to get up after falling; and can roll over, stand up, and sit down faster. A toddler loves to run.

TIP Preschooler

Taking your preschooler to the playground to play on the equipment is an important way to expose your child to lots of different movements. Using the equipment helps them to develop a sense of balance. The basis for physical functioning is established in this way. To provide a calming and a safe introduction to swinging, try holding your child tightly on your lap while slowly swinging with your feet on the ground.

Do not force your child to do anything. If your child will not participate, then realize that this may be a sign of SI problems. Think about contacting a therapist, too.

When your child has reached the age of three to four years, he or she enjoys sliding, swinging, and especially running around in circles. The child has a great need to move.

Between four and eight years, your child likes to play games in which the two of you freeze or play tag, alternated with quiet time and crafts. Playgrounds are still popular, as are riding bikes and dancing.

Between eight and twelve years, your child usually wants to play outside as much as possible. Favorite activities include football, soccer, skateboarding, and jumping rope. Your child wants to run faster, climb higher, and bike harder. He or she enjoys jumping on trampolines, going on amusement park rides that spin, and driving bumper cars. Sedentary positions—such as sitting at school or watching TV, using the computer, lying on the ground, or sitting in a crossed-legged position—are alternated with moving and playing.

TIP Homework

After school, it is better to let your child first go outside to play, bike, or take part in a sports activity. In this way, your child gets enough equilibrium stimulation to be able to sit quietly and concentrate on homework later.

TIP Teenagers

Between twelve and eighteen years, teenagers often lie on the couch for hours, in addition to playing sports after school, going on a roller coaster or other amusement park rides, and pursuing other means of inducing dizziness or thrill seeking. All of these activities are normal for teenagers. Music and dancing are especially important to teenagers. When they dance to loud music, they may move their bodies and heads in a certain manner that helps develop a finer sense of equilibrium.

A teenager between the ages of twelve and eighteen likes to spend hours talking with friends. They love to sit still, but they also love to play sports and take part in fitness activities, such as aerobics. They seek fast speeds through sports, driving, riding a motorcycle, and other activities. Teenagers are hungry for adventure and movement—whether on a wilderness expedition or through risky activities, such as bungee jumping.

TIP Adults

When you are in your thirties, you feel less need to move quickly through space. Adults still play sports, but at slower speeds and less often. Sitting for the whole day is not uncommon. Activities that include turning, such as rides at an amusement park, are less pleasurable because they can cause dizziness.

Playing sports and remaining active are not only good for your health as an adult, but they also continue to stimulate your vestibular system. This is one reason active sports make you feel better.

Problems Hyperactive Children Can Have with the Vestibular System

Hyperactive children may have vestibular systems that do not "feel" or detect changes in their sense of balance. They may require more and greater changes to really feel something is different in their bodies. Of course, all children need vestibular stimuli, but these children may seek them out more actively by moving and running, climbing, standing up frequently, moving frenetically, and turning in circles.

The vestibular system needs movement to develop. It is very important to allow your child to move so his or her sense of balance can improve. If your child needs more vestibular stimulation, and if such incessant movement is not always appreciated at home, he or she may be better off playing outside or going to the playground. Later in life, individuals who need more movement can benefit from playing sports.

The Touch System: The Sense of Feeling with the Skin

Our skin contains very tiny sensory cells. These cells provide information about the immediate environment; for example, they indicate how warm or cold it is, how rough or gentle someone's touch is, the effect of the weight of clothing or bed linens, and the perceived difference on the skin from air pressure when a door opens. We have a greater concentration of sensory cells in some areas of skin (e.g., the area around the mouth, the lips, the fingertips, and the area around the genitals) than in other areas. These areas of the body are important for survival because they are involved in the basic functions of eating, drinking, and reproduction.

The Importance of Touch

Thanks to the touch system, it is possible to feel people, animals, objects, and materials in our environment. A well-developed sense of touch is highly important for our quality of life. Especially during the first years of life, touching and being touched are important in the process of developing trust with our parents and in establishing relationships with others.

Discrimination Using Touch

Different types of sensory cells receive different kinds of information (Figure 4.5). As a result, we can distinguish varied types of pain, such as sharp or burning pain. We can feel the temperature of everything we touch; we also notice vibrations through our skin. The sensation of softness or hardness is discerned as pressure on our skin. If someone touches us, we can feel it without seeing it. Using our fingertips, it is possible to distinguish between the finest cloth and a rough material. In our mouths, we can discern something as small as a sand kernel. With our eyes closed, we can easily detect if we are in a big box full of plastic balls or in a swimming pool. Without looking, we can fasten buttons. Also, we can tell without looking whether our faces are dirty. We can even tell what kind of dirt it is; whether it is warm or cold, sticky or dry; and whether it burns. This function of the skin is called the ability to *discriminate*.

FIGURE 4.5. Most children at a certain age enjoy playing with finger paints or other gooey substances, including food. Children with problems tolerating these early touch sensations frequently have other tactile problems, as well.

Protective Touch

Another important function of the skin is protection. For example, if our skin feels too warm or too cold, our body reacts; if someone pinches us too hard, it hurts. If we notice a splinter break through the skin, we have time to protect ourselves by reacting. These reactions are the result of information that comes together in the central nervous system (Figure 4.6).

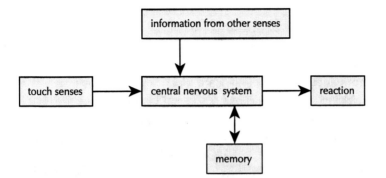

FIGURE 4.6. The primary tactile information about what, for example, your hand feels in your pocket comes from the receptors in your skin on your fingers and palms. This information is combined with information from other senses, such as kinesthesia, the information from your joints and muscles. If the object you hold jingles, the auditory information is integrated as well. Your memory is able to put all of this information to make an assessment that generates a reaction—you realize you have a key chain. Note that having no reaction is also a form of reaction.

The Normal Development of Touch

In the womb, the fetus floats in warm liquid. The skin first develops feeling around the mouth. As early as three and a half weeks into pregnancy, the fetus uses his or her mouth, fingers, and toes to explore. Fetuses have enough sensory information to find their own thumbs to suck. The palms of the hands begin to have sensation before the arms do. Feeling in the legs follows—then the tongue, the back, and the side of the trunk. After four months, the skin of the stomach and buttocks is sensitive.

Feeling in a newborn baby's skin exemplifies the protective aspect of touch. The baby reacts to changes in temperature. The skin on the baby's face is sensitive to touch. When stroked on the face, he or she reacts by looking for the mother's nipple. If you touch the toes or fingers, they react by clasping. These are reflexes, and they are necessary for survival.

As children develop, different kinds of touch are easier to discriminate. The child learns to differentiate which stimuli are acceptable, which are uncomfortable, and which are painful. Almost all babies experience the prick of a needle as painful. A dirty diaper does not bother some small children, while others find it uncomfortable. Often, the baby's cry is indicative of how it literally feels about, for example, having a dirty diaper. A baby's cry can tell parents the degree of distress the baby is experiencing in response to a particular situation.

> **TIP** **Feeling Safe**
>
> When a baby is held in a soft carrier positioned across the caretaker's chest, the baby's skin is soothed yet strongly stimulated. This type of touch provides a safe feeling. Hard plastic carriers, however, are not as well suited to the baby's sense of touch. Even when they are lined, such carriers lack the soothing quality provided by human contact. In addition, the baby is forced to remain in one position instead of having the ability to move with the rhythm of the caretaker.

From the time they are toddlers, children continue to improve their ability to discriminate. Children use information they gather from their senses. For example, a child uses the sense of touch, along with other senses, to learn how and where to place his or her hands when putting on a coat.

Problems Hyperactive Children Can Have with Touch

ADAM

Adam is a year and a half old. He is constantly moving. He touches everything. He picks up a toy and throws it away, and then is quickly in pursuit of the next activity. In this way, he is busy for the whole day without actually playing with anything. He is too busy to make contact. He almost never looks at the faces of his parents and does not like to sit in their laps. If they pick him up, he squirms himself loose. Dressing and washing him is still a battle. His forehead is wrinkled into a serious frown and he often looks angry. Adam wakes up at 5:00 A.M. and almost never naps. He may not go to sleep until after 11:00 P.M. and can wake up several times during the night. He has exhausted his parents until they are at their wits' end.

Adam does not play quietly with toys. Because he only touches them briefly before throwing them away, he never learns much about the toys. As a result, his insight into different materials is not well developed and he acquires little knowledge about the consequences of his actions. His concentration is weak. Adam derives little pleasure from playing and clearly does not feel happy.

Adam was referred to an SI-trained therapist because of sleep problems and hyperactive behavior. Through SI treatment, his body has begun to relax. His parents are actively involved in the treatment. He sleeps longer and more deeply. He is calmer, looks at things longer, has begun to play, and now occasionally comes to his parents for a hug.

The way Adam plays and behaves shows that he is trying to avoid touch stimuli and is exhibiting a negative reaction. The irritated way he reacts when he is picked up and the constant way he tries to escape being touched point to an escape behavior called flight. This behavior is also called *tactile defensiveness* or *aversion*. When he pushes away his parents, it is called *defensiveness*. Whatever it is called, this behavior causes difficulty for both the family and the child.

Hyperactive children can be oversensitive to touch, especially touch they do not expect. An ordinary touch stimulus may be perceived as threatening. The child reacts strongly to the stimulus or tries to get away from it. Both the strong reaction and the attempt to stay out of people's way can make the child act in a hyperactive manner.

However, these children also need to be touched. They prefer to seek contact themselves—for example, by going to sit on their parents' laps. The child may request snuggling or even extreme bodily contact. They chose when, for how long, and how often this physical contact lasts. But frequently, if the parent or caretaker approaches the child, it is not accepted. This is a "paradox": having a very receptive, cuddly child when the child wants it, but then the child shows defensive behavior when another approaches. This behavior is frequently seen in children hypersensitive to touch. For these children, being able to control the amount and type of stimuli is a sign to the SI therapist that the child's tactile systems are not in order.

> **TIP Water**
>
> If your child does not like to be splashed with water or to get his or her face wet, we suggest you let the child wash himself or herself. In this way, your child has control over the amount of water and the speed with which it comes out of the faucet. If desired, the child can protect his or her eyes from the water. The same holds true for washing hair. As much as possible, let your child be the one to do it. A wet washcloth held over the eyes can make the whole experience of rinsing shampoo out of the hair much more pleasant (Figure 4.7 on the next page).

In the presence of an overabundance of touch stimuli, proprioception, the feeling derived from the muscles, joints, and tendons, can be used to modify or inhibit the reaction (Figure 4.8 on the next page). Stimulating sensors in the muscles and their attaching ligaments, etc., can lessen the hypersensitivity reaction to touch. A child who is oversensitive to touch and quickly feels

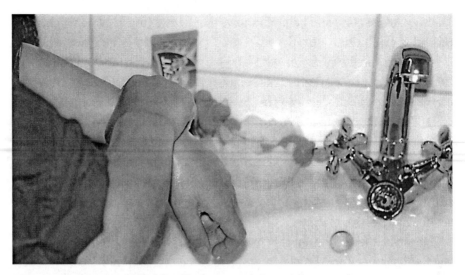

FIGURE 4.7. Soap suds feel fine if your sense of touch is normal.

threatened by it can restore balance by jumping, by throwing himself or herself at something soft (e.g., a large sofa), by playing a sport, or by becoming very active. Obviously, this is not always a happy solution, and the child can create more problems by engaging in additional overactive behavior.

In SI therapy, proprioception is often used to reduce overstimulation to the touch system. One example is jumping on a trampoline; when a child jumps on the trampoline, the vestibular system helps reduce the tactile stim-

FIGURE 4.8. Proprioception is the information or stimuli received by the brain through the sensory nerves from our muscles, joints, and tendons.

uli. Another example is applying pressure through the deep pressure techniques.[2] In this technique, which must be learned from a therapist, the skin is massaged according to a special protocol using a special brush, followed by small applications of pressure to all the joints.

At home, you can use other activities to reduce the negative effects of an inadequately functioning tactile system by wrapping your child in a blanket or even by rolling your child back and forth. A game we play for this purpose is called "making a hotdog roll." The adult can pretend to smear mustard on the outside of the blanket, using strong pressure.

Another game for applying strong pressure is called "hamburger" or "making a sandwich." This involves piling cushions on top of your child. Of course, you must leave breathing room and enough space so he or she can wiggle out. Some children need so much pressure that you can actually lie on top of them while they are under the pile of cushions. Other activities include fighting with cushions and games in which stomping and jumping are prominent.

TIP Deep Pressure

Children with problems processing tactile information can become calm when deep pressure is used. For example, deep pressure can be experienced by the children (and the caretaker) by holding the child against you in a firm but friendly way. Putting both hands firmly on a child's shoulders can be calming, particularly if the child anticipates he will be touched, by seeing you approach, or even by asking him permission. Placing a full hand firmly on a child's diaphragm, in the middle of his body just below his ribs, and breathing slowly with the child can be very calming. Teaching a child to use this type of pressure himself is very easy and effective, giving even small children a feeling of self-control and pride about their ability to calm themselves down.

Deep pressure is also experienced when playing sports or engaging in intense physical activity. Your child needs a strong trunk to be able to move his or her shoulders and hips when engaging in heavy work. To encourage the development of a strong trunk, ask your child to carry big objects, push the grocery cart, or do other heavy physical work, such as vacuuming or other household chores. For some children, even setting the table is considered heavy work. Games that help develop the heavy-work muscles include wrestling, jumping rope, and playing with heavy balls.

It can be problematic if children fulfill their need for touch by touching themselves or others in a less than desirable way. If a child keeps wriggling, picking at skin or eyelashes, or hanging onto the parents, he or she may be demonstrating a constant need for touch stimuli. You can try to replace this unacceptable behavior in such a way that the need is met in a socially acceptable behavior. For example, give your child a Koosh ball (made of rubber filaments wrapped around a center core) or some other squishy type of ball on a key chain that you attach to his or her belt loop. Teach your child to play with the ball instead of acting on the urge to wriggle or to use his or her fingers. Give your child a favorite blanket, toy, a snugly item, or a big chair with many cushions to replace hanging-on behavior. Gently massage his or her hands and/or feet.

> **TIP** **Ideas for helping your child process tactile information**
>
> ■ Let your child be the one who initiates and performs an activity (e.g., toothbrushing). If you think a better job is necessary, follow up and complete the task in a loving way.
>
> ■ Let or encourage your child to wear clothes that provide deep, smooth pressure. Clothes that are smooth to the touch and physically cool can be calming; heavy material that is tightly fitting (e.g., leotards, biking shorts) can also have this effect on some children.
>
> ■ For physical contact, a hug is better than a soft kiss. Tickles usually are not appreciated, unless your child can accept them.
>
> ■ The ability to tolerate a kiss or hug from a family member may or may not be acceptable, depending on how often your child has the opportunity to be with that person. Familiarity with the giver makes it easier for your child to accept tactile attention, because he or she can anticipate the amount and type of stimuli the kiss or hug will bring. Your child probably needs to prepare his or her nervous system for this social occurrence. However, sometimes not even a favorite aunt, grandparent, or the parent is able to kiss a child without a negative response. In this case, try having your child initiate the kiss. If this approach does not work, the child's sensory processing disorder needs to be respected, without making a big issue about the situation.[3]

The Auditory System: The Sense of Hearing

Because the ability to hear is a complicated process, we present a simplified description here. Sound is reproduced through vibrations (tremors) that are sent through the air with the help of pressure waves. A vibration moves from its source, travels through air or liquid, enters the outer ear canal, and then goes through the tympanum to the middle ear. The middle ear is made up of three bones: the hammer, anvil, and stirrup (Figure 4.9). These three bones are housed in the hardest bone system in the human skeleton because they are so sensitive and need this extra protection. From the middle ear, the vibration is sent through a thin membrane and is "felt" in the fluid around the cochlea, which resembles a curled-up shell. In the cochlea, miniscule nerve cells, in the form of hairs, send the vibration to the cerebral cortex. Nerve cells in the cortex report the sound to us. This process happens in both ears.

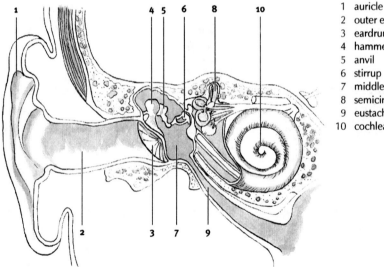

1 auricle
2 outer ear canal
3 eardrum
4 hammer
5 anvil
6 stirrup
7 middle ear
8 semicircular canal
9 eustachian tube
10 cochlea

FIGURE 4.9. The ear canal

Sounds also travel through bones. Like air vibrations, bone vibrations are sent to the cortex, where the sound is analyzed. Certain sound vibrations also help stimulate the balance system. The hearing system and the balance system strongly influence each other.[4] SI therapy makes good use of this mutual influence to further the processing of stimuli and improve auditory function.

The Importance of Hearing

Hearing and movement are closely related neurologically (Figure 4.10). The interconnection between hearing and the vestibular system is very important. The nerves in both systems are actually two parts of the same nerve complex and share certain parts in common. The way these nerves influence each other is a beautiful example of sensory integration.

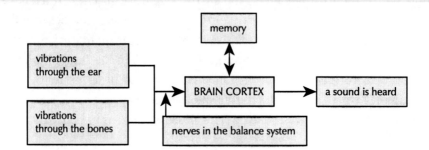

FIGURE 4.10. You hear through your ears, bones, the nerves in your inner ear, and your vestibular system. This information is analyzed in the brain's cortex.

The vestibular nerves do much to assist with hearing. They help route vibrations, which transmit information through the hair cells to enable hearing. They help achieve just the right muscle tension in the body. We know that hearing sounds is different from understanding and processing words and turning them into meaningful information.[5] Listening can be very difficult if your child is hyperactive.

Hearing well is difficult when physical problems are present, such as stuffed ears. This is common knowledge, and most doctors will frequently refer children with this problem to an ear, nose, and throat doctor for an evaluation. Some therapists also evaluate various functions related to sucking, swallowing, and tongue movements, which are related to how well one can clear one's ears when they are stuffed up. Swallowing and sucking require proper muscle tension.[6] When we swallow, the eustachian tube, which is located under each of our ears, opens and the connection between the nose, pharynx, and middle ear is facilitated. If your child does not swallow properly, the eustachian tubes could be blocked. This can increase the risk of ear problems (e.g., middle ear infections, or *otitis media*). Approximately 85 percent of all Dutch children have a middle ear infection before their fifth birthday.[7] If your child has repeated ear infections during the first year of life, hearing loss or hearing problems or balance problems can result by the time he or she is five years old. Often the hearing remains intact, but the regulatory work of the middle ear is disturbed or no longer remains entirely functional. As a result, listening and concentration can become difficult.

TIP **Ear Infections**

Ear infections are not always painful for children. The following symptoms can signal that it is time to treat an ear infection:

- Your child does not remember what you said.
- Your child no longer speaks clearly.
- Your child suddenly clings to you, hangs onto you, and has no energy.
- Your child rubs or keeps pulling on his or her ears.
- Your child holds his or her head tilted toward the side of the infection.

According to research reported in scientific journals, some ear infections can lead to a poor sense of balance on the side affected by the infection. Ear infections are said to be a major cause of attention and learning problems in certain children who are susceptible to them. Many parents of children who have frequent ear infections say that, during the time their children had infections, they were frequently hyperactive or apathetic.[8]

TIP **Soothing**

If you suspect your child has an ear infection, you may be able to soothe the child by rocking him or her gently in your arms, holding the child close to you. In this way, the balance function of the auditory nerves is also addressed. Even better is to talk to or sing to your child while holding him against you. Sounds are felt in our bones, so the child can still "hear" you, even if his or her ears are blocked.

The Normal Development of Hearing

While in the womb, the fetus hears all sorts of noises made by the mother—from the heartbeat and the breath to the processing of food and drink. The vibrations are transported through the amniotic fluid to the baby's ears, and they are also felt through the bones. One of the best positions for the bones to absorb sound is when the spinal columns of the mother and child lie close together. The mother's voice stands out across all the watery, beating, and rushing sounds. Because the baby's auditory organs are already developed by the fourth month of pregnancy, they can hear their mother's "melody." A six-month-old fetus moves to the rhythm of the mother's voice. An unborn child cannot understand what the mother is saying, but the fetus can understand the emotional content of the message. The rhythms and intonations specific to the voice of the baby's mother and the language she speaks (i.e., the language that will become the baby's mother tongue) penetrate the baby's nervous system.[9]

TIP **Pregnancy**

A happy, calm, warm, and hopeful voice encourages the fetus to learn to listen and later to communicate.

When a baby is four weeks old, he or she may be frightened by loud noises, such as the slamming of a door or the honking of a car's horn. You can see that a baby listens by looking at his or her face when the child is spoken to but cannot see the source of the words. You can also see that your baby responds to music played at a normal volume.

Gaining language skills and acquiring motor skills often go together. As soon as a baby can lift his or her head, the baby will turn toward sound. This is one of the major ways children develop the feeling for space and spatial relations. From the moment children are able to respond to sound, they notice from which direction the sound is coming. Stimulating your baby's ears with sounds and voice is naturally very important. Combining movement with voice and sounds is also important because this connects the auditory nerves and the vestibular nerves so they can support each other's functions.

In the first year of life, a child is transformed from someone who experiences the world while lying horizontally into a child who can turn around unassisted, stand up, and perhaps even walk. All movements and postures proceed in a predetermined order: Children must be able to turn before they can sit; children must be able to crawl before they can to walk. You can use these different postures and positions to stimulate your child's sense of balance, which is connected to the auditory system in the inner ear. Because of this connection, moving and balancing stimulate auditory and language development.

TIP Language

As your child learns to turn, walk, move, and take different postures, he or she not only improves the sense of balance and motor skills, but also helps activate the auditory system. This is because the sense of balance, the vestibular system, is closely connected with the auditory system. In fact, they share at least 11 connections, so movement stimulates auditory processing as well.

By the time a child has reached the age of twelve months, he or she tends to favor soft sounds. The child is soothed by a familiar voice.

By eighteen months, a toddler can often say a clear word, repeat animal sounds, and react to simple commands. If you ask something of the child, he or she may try to make the answer clear with the help of gestures.

When the child is two years old, he or she can speak sentences of several words or more. The child recognizes sounds originating in another room, such as the telephone or the doorbell. Children with good hearing consciously modify the sounds they make with their voices. Regardless of their mother tongue, all children use such sounds as *ma* and *da* or *do* to elicit a reaction from their parents. Sounds are imitated. For example, ask, "What does the train say?" Your child will answer, "Choo, choo, choo."

At nursery school age, activities such as listening to music, singing, talking, reciting poems, and playing with other children become important. These activities use sounds as well as movement, which is exactly what your child needs to develop language skills.

TIP Music

Hyperactive children often become calmer as they listen to classical music, especially by Mozart. Other kinds of music can also be soothing. Note how your child reacts to different music styles and remember what calms him or her. Use this music in the background if your child is too frenetic. Sometimes turning music *off* can also restore calm.

In kindergarten, playing games can help children learn to listen and speak clearly (Figure 4.11 on the next page). Games can help children learn to control their voices and to understand the ways they move.

Older children have to listen to their teachers to understand instructions. They receive less help in the form of pictures or visual aids (e.g., counting on

FIGURE 4.11. *Sound and movement are an important combination in the development of language.*

fingers) than do younger children. Good listeners have learned to tune out background noise and focus on the voice of their teachers.

Adolescents receive schoolwork that requires reading and abstract thinking. When students talk to each other about this work, their hearing systems can help strengthen their understanding of abstract information.

TIP   School

If your child can hear a book being read aloud by a parent, caretaker, or teacher at the same time he or she is reading it, the child may find it easier to absorb and assimilate the words. If your child can first think about a text and then hears his or her voice repeat the information, the child's comprehension can improve. This works well with homework, too.

As a child becomes older, his or her ability to hear high tones diminishes. Walkmen and MP3 players with volumes that are set too high can cause hearing damage. Loud noises can also damage hearing and reduce the ability to hear high tones.

TIP   Rest

When your child is resting, it is a good idea to minimize noise in the immediate area. Always turn off the television when no one is watching.

Problems Hyperactive Children Can Have with Hearing and Communication

JACK

Jack, who is eight years old, asked, "Dad, can I please water the garden?

His dad replied, "Okay, but don't make the terrace wet. And make sure no water lands in the pots because then they get much too wet. And be sure to keep the water away from the windows."

Because Jack said nothing, his father made the assumption he had listened. Jack picked up the garden hose and wet everything his father had just forbidden him to water.

Sometimes a child with an attention problem does not really understand the spoken message. Jack was so excited he could spray the garden that he did not pay attention to exactly what his father said. Even though his father used words an eight-year-old could understand, he probably used too many sentences. Jack was already preoccupied. He was so preoccupied with exactly what he would do that he did not process all his father's words. In his wound-up state, Jack was not able to process the stimulus—his father's message. His father could have said, "Jack, listen carefully. Only the grass can get wet. Nothing else. Tell me, what can get wet?" After Jack had given the correct answer, his father could have turned over the hose.

Likewise, a child whose level of arousal is too high will probably not be able to hear what his or her parent is saying. Talking to the child probably will not help at this moment. But helping him or her to stop running around, being calm yourself, and slowing your own breathing can help. Try using a calm, soft voice to slow down the physical action, and give your child a chance to self-regulate. At this point, you could say you prefer that your child "set your motor at a lower speed" or "turn your engine off." This is part of the philosophy of Williams and Schellenburg's *How Does Your Engine Run?* program. Children can relate to this kind of language and consider it a game. This program is discussed in the section covering therapy (see Chapter 5).

TIP Attention

First, calm your child down so he or she can listen. Say what you have to say in a few sentences and use words that are easy to process. Ask your child to repeat what you said so you know he or she heard the message and understands it.

The Visual System: The Sense of Sight

Our visual system involves the functions of both looking and seeing. *Looking* and *seeing* mean different things. Looking uses the eyes to gather information. Seeing refers to forming an image in the brain. More happens in the brain during the seeing process than in the looking process. The visual system can be described as the queen of the sensory systems (Figure 4.12). It has an important effect on the processing of stimuli from the other senses, and it can dominate those other senses.

FIGURE 4.12. Vision is the process of identifying images, understanding what the eyes see, and preparing to respond.[10]

Think of the following situation: You are sitting in a train that is not moving and another train starts moving next to you. You think you are moving because your eyes interpret motion from the information they have been given. In fact, the muscles of your eyes have been tricked into this confusion. The visual system tells the motion receptors in the ears that movement is taking place, and stimuli are sent to the muscles; you think you have started moving. The motion sensors in the muscles and joints (i.e., the proprioceptors) provide that sensation of movement.

The Importance of Sight

Sight is important because it serves a variety of critical functions. It can warn us, and it can orient us to our environment. It also serves in emotional, language, and motor skill development. It plays a key role in how we experience our world.

Warning and Orientation

As is the case with the other sensory systems, the most important function of the visual system is to warn us about danger. It warns us if a dangerous object comes too close.

Visual information can help us orient ourselves in space; that is, it lets us know where we are and how far away we are from specific objects. If an object comes closer, we can see that it is closer. By combining the images with sound stimuli, it is possible to estimate the speed at which something is approaching and from which direction it will arrive.

Emotional, Language, and Motor Skills Development

The visual system also helps us form an image in our brain of how things feel (Figure 4.13). A good example is when a child sees a toy and touches it. When the child sees the toy, he or she combines the visual information with how it feels to touch it and perhaps how it feels in his or her mouth. The stimuli from the taste sensors in the mouth, from the muscle movement sensors in the fingers, and the image of what the toy looks like are combined until the baby learns it is a square wooden toy, even though he or she cannot yet describe it. This process of seeing, feeling, and manipulating with the mouth and both hands forms the basis of later school readiness.[11] Children are only ready for school when they know and recognize basic forms; for example, a child is ready for school when he or she recognizes an apple in a picture, has an image of what an apple feels like, knows what one can do with an apple, and knows how an apples tastes and what colors it can be.

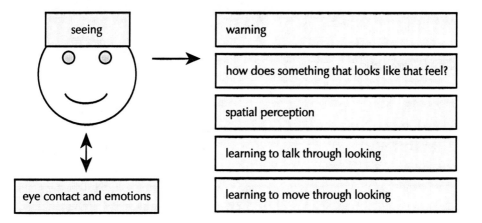

FIGURE 4.13. What you see is very important to your ability to function.

Language development is promoted when a child stares intently at the mouth and facial expressions of the speaker. A baby enjoys doing this and thus learns to combine sounds with the movements of the mouth. This is a complex interaction, and one that is crucial for mimicking the mouth movements required when learning to speak.

The eyes play an important role in the development of motor skills. If a baby is lying in a crib with a mobile hanging above it, and accidentally touches the mobile, he or she will then have two primary sensory systems working: vision and touch. The baby thinks this is a funny effect, so he or she keeps repeating the arm movement that caused the mobile to move. In this way, the baby learns to coordinate movement patterns into fluid—but more importantly, purposeful—motions (see Figure 4.14).

FIGURE 4.14. This baby is playing with a mobile.

Visual Perception

The ability to perceive and interpret and to understand what our eyes see is called *visual perception*.[12] If the baby cited in the above example sees the mobile again, he or she may try to touch it, especially if the infant recognizes it as a mobile. The conscious action the baby takes to touch the mobile is called a *motor plan*. A motor plan allows us to chart or determine how to move so we can reach a goal. This plan takes place in a circuit in the brain. That circuit can be changed slightly to meet the next challenge, such as how to touch the mobile if it is hanging at a different level.

Experiencing the World

We use our brains to plan how we will use our bodies. We look at the execution and effects of our movements just as the baby in the above example observed and touched the mobile. Four systems are involved in defining the image: the visual (seeing the toy), the tactile (touching the toy), the proprioceptive (movement and feeling the position of the arms and hands), and the auditory (listening to the sound it makes). This is how we learn to experience the world. A baby learns about timing, space, and cause and effect through these playful discoveries.

Eye Contact and Security

In many cultures, when two people are talking and expressing emotions, they look into each other's eyes. For centuries, making eye contact has been lauded in poetry and other literature as a sign of openness. The attachment and attunement needs of an infant are dependent on eye contact, usually with their primary caretaker. The attachment and attunement ability of a baby is the most important factor in developing a safe bond. Babies are completely open. If you are admiring a newborn, it can be disappointing if the baby's eyes are closed. Eye contact is one of the many joyful exchanges you can have with a newborn. The open way in which babies and mothers look into each other's eyes is similar to the eye contact in an open, honest conversation. This may be why people do everything they can to get a baby to look at them: make noises, shake a rattle, or hold the baby in a different way. Babies also seem interested in making eye contact when they are hungry, have a dirty diaper, need to be soothed, or are curious.

A sensitive adult can read a lot in a child's eyes. The adult's own eyes can transfer the basis for a child's sense of security, the feeling of being loved, the feeling people are trustworthy, and the confidence that the child has the ability to function in daily life.

The Normal Development of Sight

After birth, the size of a baby's eyes does not increase, but vision improves. Babies can see, but not in a detailed way. The ability to coordinate eye movements has not yet developed, but the baby can distinguish figures moving in the immediate surroundings. Depth perception is not yet possible because it requires too much coordination between both eyes.

> ### TIP Learning to Look
>
> To exercise your baby's eyes, encourage him or her to look in different directions. You can accomplish this by moving the crib around the room. If light comes from different directions, your baby will look toward those directions, thus learning to use both eyes. Alternate the arm on which you carry your baby so he or she can learn to use both eyes at the same time.

Focusing on the face of a parent or caregiver is a very important step when a baby is learning to focus. Babies find it especially easy to recognize the hair and hairline of their caretakers. While a baby is being hugged or fed, his or her eyes focus carefully on the parent's face. Even a two-month-old baby will expect to see and can imitate certain facial expressions.

As babies grow older, they are better able to control their eye movements. The baby begins to recognize stationary objects as well as moving ones. The baby can clearly see your face when you are feeding him or her. The baby first learns how satisfying it is to suck from a nipple and later learns how that nipple looks. The baby quickly anticipates nursing when he or she sees a bottle or breast.

> ### TIP Looking
>
> The most ideal location for toy placement is eight to ten inches away from your baby's eyes. Changing the distance your baby's mobile hangs is also good for learning about space. Hanging it where the baby can touch it is good; alternatively, placing it about three feet away provides another type of stimuli. Combine different stimuli; for example, shake the rattle as you move it back and forth before your baby's eyes. Tell your baby you are giving him or her the toy, even if the baby is not yet able to grab it.

Between the fourth and sixth months, toys that involve both visibility and movement are still recommended. There are many baby books available. It is good for babies to listen and look at pictures. They see how the pages turn and learn which sounds belong with which pictures. In this way, an understanding of reading is established.

> ### TIP Playing
>
> Games, such as teaching your baby to clap, help improve eye-hand co-ordination.

In the period between six and eight months, a baby begins to move around. This is the beginning of real cooperation between the visual system and the other senses. The baby sees something, goes after it, and feels it with his or her hands.

The closer the baby gets to an object, the bigger the object's image is when projected on the retina of the baby's eyes. The images are received through the senses and delivered to the brain. The brain "sees" that the image is getting larger as the baby moves toward it. This way, the baby learns about the surrounding space and develops spatial insight.

As babies grow, they learn to fixate on objects with their eyes. They can direct their eyes toward something or alternate focusing on one object and then another. Playing with toys teaches children how to move their fingers and hands well and how to manipulate objects. This happens while the child is looking at what he or she is doing. This is an important developmental phase in the development of eye-hand coordination.

TIP Creeping

You can help develop your baby's ability to crawl. Place your baby stomach down on your lap and let him or her reach for and play with a toy that lies next to you. You can sit on the couch or on the ground. This stimulates the development of the strong neck and back required for crawling and head lifting, and it definitely helps your baby look at things with well-coordinated eyes. To make certain that his or her neck and back are not becoming too tired, change positions now and then (Figure 4.15).

FIGURE 4.15. Lifting the baby's head stimulates the back muscles.

When babies lie on their backs and play with their feet, they develop an idea about how long they are. These activities also help with motor coordination. Games and toys that encourage babies to look, move, and feel may help them form a positive self-image at later stages in their lives. At a very young age, babies derive pleasure from looking at the movements of their hands and at activities such as dropping toys.

Problems Hyperactive Children Can Have with Sight

Hyperactive children can have problems "seeing the trees for the forest." If these children look in a pile of rubbish, they will not find the one item they want to find. On a full piece of paper, they may fail to find the math sum on which they just worked.

TIP **Oversight**

Providing an organized room for your child at home can be very helpful. In an organized room, he or she can see the toy for which he was looking. Structure is, in general, good for these children. In school, the important math problem a child cannot solve can be easier to figure out if it is written on a blank sheet of paper or on a sheet with blocks for each problem.

Some children can be oversensitive to light. They are calmer when the light is dimmed. The fluorescent lamps in most classrooms can be too bright and very annoying, especially if flickering. On the other hand, some children prefer be in bright light and become restless in soft light.

The Proprioceptive System: The Sense of Feeling in the Muscles and Joints

Our bodies are made up of a skeleton of bones that are fastened together with cartilage, ligaments, and tendons. The connection between two or more bones is called a joint. Tendons are used to attach muscles to bone.

As a muscle begins to contract, it becomes wider and shorter; it then moves the bone to which it is attached. To carry out an ordinary movement (e.g., picking up a bag), several muscles from one group must contract while others must relax. All of this must take place at the right moment. To maintain a particular position, some muscles must be tensed while others must either be equally tense or relax somewhat. At the instant when a muscle is moving, sensory signals proceed to the spine and to the brain. Through the influence of gravity and through small changes in position (e.g., turning the head), the muscles are constantly busy trying to maintain general balance or perhaps maintaining the same position. Think about how difficult it is to sit up straight for a long time or to stay standing on both legs without shifting your weight from one leg to the other.

The sensory receptors in our joints, tendons, and cartilage, along with the gravity receptors in the vestibular system, provide us with information concerning our posture and how to change it when needed. A movement can only be well executed if the nervous system can relay accurate information about the current position of the body to the spine and the brain. All the muscles and joints are constantly sending information about the condition of the body. This happens through very small proprioceptive receptors, or sensors, in the skin, sinews, muscle fibers, ligaments, and cartilage. These sensors supply the sensation of posture and movement.

The Importance of the Proprioceptive System

Our proprioceptive system is sometimes called the *hidden sensory system* because it is embedded in our muscles, joints, and tendons and is not really obvious on the outside of the body. But if we did not have this extremely important sense, we would literally fall down. It provides a foundation for everything from posture, to how to put your arm in your sleeve behind your back, to helping you "feel" the correct finger when you are typing text without looking at your hands.

A Sense of How You Carry Yourself

The small sensory cells in the muscles enable each of us to feel the way we carry and move our bodies (Figure 4.16 on the next page). Without this feeling, it would also not be possible to make supple movements or to remain standing, sitting, or lying in the same position. We must continuously correct ourselves by making postural adjustments. In general, these corrections happen automatically, without our needing to think about them. Although many sensors exist in the trunk and legs, the greatest concentration of proprioceptive receptors is found in the eye muscles, hand muscles, and neck muscles. Because of this heavy concentration, it is not surprising that these areas contribute to good eye-hand coordination.

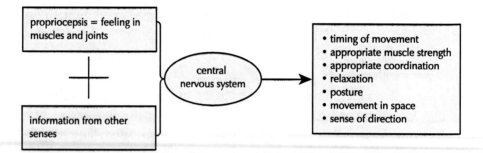

FIGURE 4.16. A good sense of feeling in your muscles and joints is an important factor in being able to move well.

Coordination with Other Sensory Systems

Vision is an important part of the ability to move well. If we look at our surroundings or at ourselves in a mirror, it is easier for us to move, especially if we are trying a new movement. For example, it is easier to practice a new dance step in front of a mirror than it is without that visual feedback. When we are learning to execute fine movements, we constantly look at our hands.

Hearing also helps heighten our sense of spatial orientation. If we close our eyes and ears, we must rely completely on proprioception and trust our sense of balance. Try it. Place a blindfold on yourself, place your fingers in your ears, stand up, and then walk around. You may notice that you become unsure of yourself and your movements become awkward and stiff.

Another important sense affecting how we carry ourselves and move is the vestibular system. The sense of balance informs us about the position of our heads in space, whether we are moving or not, and where we are. This information is essential for the correct combination of muscle tension and relaxation needed for smooth movements.

The sense of smell and taste also influence how we carry ourselves and move. Think about how you "follow your nose" when you smell something delicious. Your head seems to drift forward. If you anticipate a familiar smell, you may take a deep breath to make room for it in your lungs. The opposite reaction can be seen in how you move when you encounter something that does not smell pleasant. The muscles in your face form a grimace. You might pull your head away from the smell and tense your neck and back muscles. You might even close your nostrils. Then you might want to leave the scene quickly—to do this, you would need to use your trunk, arms, and leg muscles to turn and walk away.

It is obvious that, in the case of posture and movement, all the senses work together to present the clearest possible image to the brain. The information received from the proprioceptors is compared with information coming in from other systems. In a sense, the brain forms an inner map, a picture of the world inside the head. In this way, a command signal can be compared with the image and eventually be sent with it to the muscles so they move in the appropriate manner.[13]

The Normal Development of the Proprioceptive System

A baby's joints move in the womb in much the same way they will later in life. After birth, babies move noticeably less actively. Once they come under the influence of gravity, all movement must be learned anew. At first, the baby is not yet ready to lift his or her head or to support the weight of the head unassisted. Therefore, the head must be cradled. The baby receives sensory information when the arms and legs bend and stretch a little or the hands open and close.

> **TIP Rest**
>
> Swaddling and holding your baby in a firm yet friendly way can frequently calm a newborn.

Eye-hand coordination begins to develop when the baby starts to look at his or her own hands, especially when moving. Being able to lift the head off the bed when lying on his or her back, and later lifting up the head when lying stomach down, are the start of developing good motor skills. Placing your baby stomach down can encourage using the neck muscles to lift the head. This is a very important developmental step that is sometimes overlooked because of our tendency to place babies in carriers.

> **TIP Learning to Move Well**
>
> Place your baby stomach down and try to attract his or her attention with sounds, games, and delicious aromas. The baby will turn his or her head in that direction, which stimulates the sensors in the neck muscles. This is also very important for exercising the neck and back muscles and for developing good eye-hand coordination. Playing on the stomach is important for exercising the neck, back, shoulder girdle, eyes, and hands.

Only when a baby's neck and trunk muscles are strong, and he can support the weight of his or her head, is it appropriate to rock your baby. It can be dangerous to use a baby bouncer if your baby's neck muscles are not strong enough to support the head.

Through repeating all sorts of different postures and movements, the sensory information in the joints and muscles gives the baby a sense of his or her body. Crawling takes on a central role in the development of motor skills because it involves coordinating both sides of the body in opposing ways: The left side stretches as the right bends. The left side of our body is controlled by the right half of our brain, and vice versa. By moving both parts of the body in a fluid and cooperative way, connections are made between both parts of the brain, which coordinates the signals (Figure 4.17).

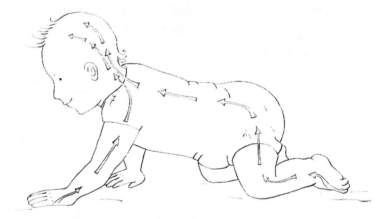

FIGURE 4.17. During the act of crawling, continuous signals are sent from the arms and legs to the brain.

Large movements stimulate many sensors in the muscles and joints. Playing with cushions, balls, and other large materials helps develop the sense of movement, proprioception.

TIP **Becoming Agile**

Large toys, such as balls and cushions, encourage large movements. During these large movements, many proprioceptors are stimulated. The development of good muscle control forms the basis for later use of gross motor skills.

Fine motor skills (i.e., precise movements of the hands and fingers) can develop properly when the muscles in the trunk are strong enough to hold a child in certain stable positions. For example, it is not possible for a child to learn to write before he or she can sit with a stable back and hold the shoulders and elbows in the position for writing. However, this capability comes quickly when all the sensory information is being processed efficiently.

At elementary-school age, children like to play outside, which mostly involves gross (i.e., large) motor activities, such as running, stopping, throwing, falling, and jumping. This is part of learning the basic motor patterns. These activities are necessary to form a good basis for more advanced motor abilities and even for developing fine motor skills, such as writing.

TIP **Preventing Injuries**

Having a good sense of the muscles and joints can help prevent injuries later in life. Let your child play outside in the yard or on the playground as much as possible. This can help him or her develop properly and can boost self-confidence.

Preteens and teenagers grow quickly and sometimes experience pain in their joints. It is a good idea to keep them moving, even though they experience growing pains. However, at times, they may have to forsake playing some sports for awhile.

Adults have a tendency to sit too much. If you work at a sedentary job, it is very important to move as much as you can during your free time. This way, your body remains supple and you help prevent heart and circulatory problems. Plus, movement is important to the upkeep of your vestibular system, and as you get older, you may need this system, which helps you know how to react to stumbles and possible falls.

Problems Hyperactive Children Can Have with the Proprioceptive System

Children with a poor awareness of their muscles and joints can be clumsy and may have a greater chance of injuries, such as sprains and joint problems, compared with children who are more agile and aware of how their bodies work. The other senses—primarily vision—may try to compensate for poor muscle and joint awareness, but this is tiring and uses up a great deal of energy. What happens is that the child needs to spend extra energy cognitively "working" on balance, rather than doing so on "automatic pilot," through the operation of the proprioceptive system.

A child with problems in the proprioceptive system can be unstable, unsure, and afraid of heights or of speed. By applying pressure in the joints and doing movements that involve heavy work (e.g., swinging, pushing a wheelbarrow, or crawling out of a "sandwich" made with cushions), a child can improve the sense of proprioception and even improve muscle power.

In SI therapy, muscle-enhancing activities can be offered during a game chosen by the child, without the child knowing he or she is undertaking a therapeutic activity. For example, today, George decides to build a tower. "Good idea," says his SI therapist. "Why don't we use the big blocks? They are great for this tower." In a little while, she places a chair nearby so George can climb. She stands next to the chair for safety and keeps adding muscle-strengthening movement into the game. George is completely absorbed in his game and has no idea that anything else is going on—certainly not muscle-building exercises.

Hyperactive children often have poor muscle tone. You might feel a limp hand in yours when walking hand-in-hand with the child and feel as though you are dragging him or her along. When you lift up children who have low or poor muscle tone, they feel extremely heavy. When these children are tired, they may bump into things. They may use too much force when roughhousing or playing. Children with poor muscle tone certainly get less and frequently inadequate information from their proprioceptive sensors.

The Sense of Smell and Taste

Two different senses are involved in the perception of taste and smell. Often the two senses are perceived as a single system because they work together to process stimuli in the mouth. The taste and smell systems both process chemical stimuli.

The senses of taste and smell work together to detect the flavor of food. The taste of what is eaten goes through the mouth to the nasal cavity, where the nerves are stimulated (Figure 4.18). If you close your eyes and pinch your nostrils shut, you cannot taste the difference between a raw apple and a potato.[14] Smell is so important because it helps trigger the memory of a taste. Actually, smell is 25,000 times stronger than taste.

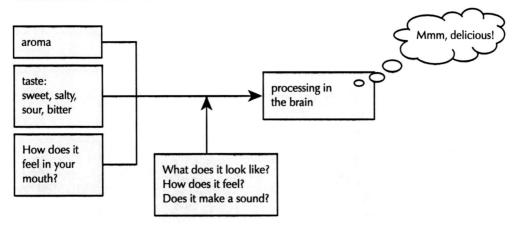

FIGURE 4.18. Is it delicious?

Smell

You can see what an instinctive system the sense of smell is by observing a baby's reaction to various smells. From the very first day of birth, a baby can recognize its mother by her smell. The sense of smell is able to determine behavior before the hearing and visual systems can. You can see from the facial expressions of a baby who is approximately fifteen hours old if he or she finds a particular smell appealing or repulsive. It can be noticed in the infant's suckling, licking of the lips, or the relaxation of facial features. Or, the baby will make a contorted face at an unpleasant smell. This instinctive reaction is registered in a part of the brain known as the *limbic system*. It helps the baby determine if something is edible.

The sense of smell has four important functions:

1. It offers protection.

2. It offers an important component to emotional and sexual life.

3. It helps jog memory because odors are stored in the memory.

4. It helps acquire food and drink.

More sensory cells are involved in smelling than in tasting. About a million cells are bundled in two membranes behind the bridge of the nose. This is a very small area, about as big as your thumbnail, but if it were spread out flat, it might well be bigger than the total area of your skin. Only 2 percent of the air we breathe travels along these cells, but our nose is so sensitive that this area can detect the smallest (a millionth of a millionth of a gram) of fragrance.

Everything we can smell is based on seven primary smells (Figure 4.19). A molecule with a certain form can activate a cell on a nose hair in the nasal passage.

FIGURE 4.19. With a good sense of smell, you can distinguish 10,000 different smells, and all these smells are combinations of the seven basic smells.

Taste

How do we know how something tastes? Our sensory receptors receive only a few molecules of a certain material. Sensory receptors for taste and smell are always damp, in order to be able to capture these fragments. The tongue, the gums, the palate, the lips, and the inside of the mouth have sensors to sample taste as well as sensors for pressure stimuli, known as *somato-sensory* receptors. These are often located next to the taste buds in the mouth and throat. In this way, we can notice touch, pressure, moisture, warmth, cold, and other properties of food, such as texture (e.g., rough, fine, round or jagged, grainy or smooth). All of these properties help determine the taste of food.

The chemicals of aromas are combined with bits of air and are noticed by the nose. The chemicals that help determine taste are bonded with certain amounts of water in food and drink. The taste sensors (i.e., the cells that receive taste stimuli) are found on the tongues of babies and young children. Adults also have taste sensors on the top of the mouth (palate), on the tonsils, and in the throat. These small sensors for chemicals form a surface similar to that on the skin of an orange. You can see them as tiny bumps and depressions on the side of the tongue. These small bumps are called *taste buds*. Adults have about nine thousand of these taste buds, and babies have many more. Older people only have about five thousand taste buds because some die off over the years. Unfortunately, the taste buds that survive have fewer chemical sensors.

Taste buds are covered with skin, but they have a small hole that permits the entry of dissolved chemical materials. The chemicals are received through the sensors, and a chemical reaction takes place that corresponds with the stimulation of one of four primary flavors: sweet, salty, sour, and bitter. In this way, the nervous system is stimulated. Every taste bud can stimulate twenty-to-thirty thousand nerve fibers. Taste buds have a short lifespan of only ten days, and they are replaced within twelve hours.

Naturally, many more flavors and food types can be distinguished in combinations of the basic four flavors. Different codes and combinations of taste signals are used to distinguish flavors in our brain. The taste buds for sweet food and drink (e.g., strawberry flavor) are found on the very tip of the tongue. On the front portion of the tongue, salty foods (e.g., potato chips) are noticed. In the middle of the tongue, sour flavors (e.g., lemon) are noticed, and on the back of the tongue, you can find the taste buds that notice bitter flavors (e.g., Brussels sprouts). In general, children prefer sweet flavors and only learn to appreciate bitter flavors later in life.

Specific brain nerves transport information about taste to the middle section of the brain. The information arrives at the brain's switching station, the thalamus. After receiving primary and secondary taste information from the cortex, the brain combines the information with more complicated information arriving via the sense of smell. Thus, what we eventually experience as the sensation of flavor is actually a combination of taste and smell.

TIP Appetite

To stimulate your baby's appetite, gently massage his or her gums.

The Importance of Smell and Taste

Eating and drinking are essential to life. Smell and taste play an important role in how we ingest the right foods. The taste and smell senses serve two important functions.

The most important function directs us to eat what we find delicious and deem to be nourishing. This is called a *discriminating* function: We are able to make a distinction between the many different flavors, smells, and forms of food and drink. Smell, as well as flavor, plays an important role in awakening the feeling of hunger. The centers that govern the positive feelings of touch, positive body sensations in general, and pleasure are found next to the taste center in the brain. The hypothalamus (which plays a major role in feeling satiated and in controlling feelings of hunger) and the limbic system (which is involved in producing emotions) are also connected to the taste and smell sensory systems. This is why taste and smell not only influence the feeling of hunger but also stimulate emotions and feelings.

Secondly, taste and smell have a protective function. Imagine a mushroom with a bizarre flavor. This strange flavor is compared in the brain's memory bank with other known flavors. An adult would probably set the mushroom aside and not eat it. However, a child would react in a more primitive way—taste the mushroom and then immediately spit it out. Both adult and child react in the correct ways to protect their bodies. They do so by recognizing that strange, often bitter, flavors may not be good for their health.

Everything the tongue perceives is smelled though the sensory cells of the nose. The eyes also help control exactly what is placed into the mouth. "Is that edible? Do I know it?" A piece of pie looks appealing, and the aroma of the pie is combined with the sensation of flavor in the mouth.

TIP   Tastes that Induce a Sense of Well-Being

Why is it that lovers of spicy food do not hate the burning sensation of some foods, such as jalapeño peppers? This is actually not a taste sensation, but rather a type of pain sensation. The pain sensors notice the chemical ingredient capsaicin. The signal travels via the trigeminal nerve to the brain. Through this process, sweet and sharp flavors are intensified and endorphins are released. Endorphins are the body's natural painkillers: As soon as endorphins enter our bloodstream, we get a feeling of well-being and pleasure. Therefore, the peppers added to spicy Mexican,

Thai, and Indian dishes give more flavor to the food and can give us a good feeling.[15]

The Normal Development of Smell and Taste

Before birth, a baby tastes the amniotic fluid in the mother's womb. Both the taste and smell sensory systems are well developed by birth. The baby can distinguish between the smell of his or her mother's breast milk and that of other mothers' milk. Later, children generally prefer sweet flavors, and many children could happily live on candy and soda.

TIP Healthy Eating

Candy, chips, soda, and fruit juice may seem like an easy way to keep children "sweet." To prevent this preference for sweet food from reducing interest in more nutritious food, try to keep such foods to a minimum. These foods are also very bad for the teeth.

You can control your child's consumption of sweet foods with some of the following strategies:

- If you put your baby to bed with a bottle, fill it with water rather than juice.
- Do not pack sweet snacks in your child's school lunch box; alternatives such as raisins and apples cut into small pieces are better for your child.
- Associate sweets with specific situations only. You can say, "At home, you get to have desserts when the adults are having them, as part of your after-school snack, or at a birthday party." Save sweets as rewards for especially difficult situations (e.g., getting your child dressed for an important appointment when he or she would rather keep playing a game). Even then, offer sweets sparingly.
- Serve fruit juice rather than soda. Save soda for festive occasions.
- Sugar-free chewing gum can help calm a hyperactive child.

In the first years of life, children learn to recognize more and more tastes and smells. Some children find a wide range of food palatable, while others do not. Some children have definite preferences and aversions for specific foods, and other children will eat whatever is put in front of them.

Each child's sense of taste and smell develops at his or her own pace, and each child develops preferences for smells he or she enjoys. Children learn to recognize smells associated with danger, such as fire. Smells can also form a large part of the memories of events and emotions.

TIP **Aromas**

Essential oils can determine the mood in a room. Many types of these oils are available, each with its own effect. Lavender is well known for its calming effect. Watch out, however, because some children are oversensitive to perfume and even to the scent of deodorants or body gels.

Problems Hyperactive Children Can Have with Smell and Taste

VANCE

From the time Vance was about two years old, he and his brother came to visit me, his stepmother, about once every two weeks. During mealtimes, he would spit out certain types of food. It seemed strange that he could walk around eating slices of apple (he liked to puree the apple in his mouth and then swallow it) but could not eat warm food at the dining room table. He was crazy about hard cookies. I thought he might be doing this for attention, so every time he spat something out, I made him leave the table. First, I moved his chair from the table, then I made him stand in the hall, and eventually he was sent to his room for spitting out his food.

This ritual lasted for some time. We tried to ignore it and hoped it was a phase. Vance was very choosy and usually preferred soft, pureed foods and carbohydrates.

Years later, when Vance was fourteen, an observant woman noticed the strange way he kept food in his cheeks. I suddenly saw him with different eyes—not as his stepmother, but as an SI therapist. Had I missed something? I checked his reflexes for gagging. Normally, these reflexes originate in the back of the mouth. I found Vance had a reflex on one side of his tongue, right beside his molars. That was why he had so much difficulty swallowing food and keeping it in his mouth. The spitting out was not attention-seeking behavior. I felt upset that I had punished him, and I told him so and apologized. I asked if he wanted to do some exercises to reduce the problem. He did and he practiced the exercises for a short time. Now he eats everything and has grown into a healthy, strapping young man.

Problems with Taste, Difficult Eating Behavior

Problems with taste can have different causes.[16] Flavor and texture, or how the food feels, are two important aspects of eating. The problems that confront both speech and occupational therapists usually have more to do with the act of eating, but sometimes the smell and texture of food is also a factor in eating problems. Low muscle tone in the tongue and a poor kinesthetic sense of awareness are usual problem areas when it comes to chewing. Eating is so important that eating problems often have emotional ramifications. It is can be a nightmare for the parents if their child will not eat. Parents often become very emotional over a child's eating behavior. Besides the health of your child, nourishment is possibly the most important issue you will face.

The first step in normalizing a problem eating situation is to find out why your child is not eating. If eating behavior does not improve quickly, your child's growth and health can be affected.[17] If your child is eating inappropriately, he or she is at risk for becoming overweight. Your child may also be at risk for long-term problems (e.g., vitamin deficiency), which can further negatively affect his or her behavior.

The underlying problem can be of a neurological or physical nature. Some children have a combination of eating disorders; for example, they may not be able to suck or swallow properly or their breathing may not be efficient. The child's appetite may be affected if he or she was not able to develop the sense of taste during the early stages of life. Working with an SI therapist or a speech therapist especially trained in eating problems can make a world of difference for these children.

TIP   Learning to Eat

Try to determine if your child has a negative reaction or an aversion to the taste or the texture of a particular food. Does your child hate food with strong flavors? Does he or she prefer sweet flavors or foods with a smooth texture? Can your child swallow normally? Or is chewing food well the problem?

To help your child expand the range of food he or she will eat, try adding herbs to sharpen the flavor, softening the flavor with mashed potatoes or milk, sweetening the food with applesauce, or cutting up the food very finely. Then introduce small samples of the "difficult" food. When your child has started eating a wider variety of foods, you will have to make fewer adjustments to his or her diet. Eating more varied foods is important for your child's health, and, of course, doing so can help develop the sense of taste.

Problems with Smell

Some children do not perceive smells well. This problem involves a portion of the olfactory system. A child with this type of problem is at a disadvantage when it comes to understanding his or her environment. Medical clinicians can provide a good diagnosis, which can help solve or reduce the problem.

Olfactory problems also can happen when someone has an accident or a physical problem with the nose. Another important problem with this sense is an aversion to a certain smell or smells. Smell aversion has been described this way: "It's not unusual for a young child to display a strong aversion to certain scents; in normal development, these reactions to smell evolve into a more comprehensive, negative reaction that is more selective."[18]

A child who displays an avoidant behavior for smells can display strong primitive reactions. The child may repeat that something or someone "stinks." The parents usually are very embarrassed by this reaction. The child reacts in an exaggerated way to the smell of certain foods, bathroom smells, body smells, and even some smells he or she does not yet recognize. These smells can be very distracting to the child. Furthermore, this behavior can make it hard for the child to be accepted socially by other children or adults.

The aversion to smells often is associated with oversensitivity to taste and auditory stimuli. SI therapy tries to normalize such sensory processes so the child receives the proper information and learns to perceive it in a normal way.

Chapter 5

SI Therapy

Materials for all the sensory systems are available at SI therapy clinics. Vestibular information for movement, tactile information for feeling, and proprioceptive information for muscle strength are three of the most important areas of input to help the child's development.

THE PURPOSE OF SI THERAPY is to improve your child's ability to process and organize sensory information. When the brain can organize sensory information, the result includes improvement in functioning, life skills, emotional development, and general development.[1] SI therapy is not about teaching new skills to your child; rather, it helps your child's brain develop processes that lay the foundation for life skills. A very important advantage is that SI therapy is playful and exploratory in nature.

This therapy can be conducted by an SI-trained occupational therapist, physical therapist, or speech therapist. SI therapy usually takes place one-on-one with the therapist and child. In some cases, parents sit in on a session and play a role in the therapy. Sometimes they arrive at the end of a session to see what has taken place, and the child is usually very proud to show what he or she has been doing.

During SI therapy, the child and therapist actively "play" together. This play is directed primarily by the child. An important characteristic of SI therapy is that it is a child-directed therapy. This means the child conveys to the therapist in words, deeds, or actions what he or she needs in terms of development or organization.

Your child is given enough space to play out his or her own ideas and is allowed to convey whatever he or she needs to fully develop. Dr. Ayres called this need for exploration the child's *inner drive*.[2] This is an extremely important therapeutic technique in SI therapy. Without it, the therapy would not qualify as sensory integration. Of course, if a child is very chaotic or is totally unable to make decisions that are purposeful, he or she must be carefully guided by the therapist, who draws upon that child's inner drive as much as possible. When a child has ownership of or an emotional investment in SI therapy, that child's brain works in a manner that results in good integration and noticeable progress.

In the home, however, a child cannot always explore everything, due to safety issues. Parents can usually take the principles of child-directed SI therapy and adopt a child-oriented approach to child rearing.

The Adaptive Response and SI Therapy

An *adaptive* response is the appropriate response to stimuli of a person's inner or outer environment.[3] When a baby sees the mother's face, for example, the infant may make an adaptive response by waving his or her arms or making gurgling sounds. In general, adaptive responses help the brain to become more organized by responding appropriately to a stimulus or situation. Adaptation helps the child achieve success with personal goals.[4]

SEBASTIAN

Sometimes a small amount of help is necessary for a child to achieve success. My one-year-old grandson, Sebastian, wanted to put a cap on a jar and then take it off. He made at least twenty attempts without success. I could see he needed just a little bit of help to make the finely tuned adjustment to get the cap on. By giving him this assistance, I helped him achieve an adaptive response. This skill became part of his repertoire of motor learning behaviors. Repetition is also crucial for development. Sebastian now has a more accurate feeling in his joints and in the muscles of his arms and hands because he went on to practice the skill correctly and made modifications when necessary.

SI therapy promotes an adaptive response in a therapeutic setting. As SI therapy improves the ways in which a child's brain combines, integrates, and processes information, the child is better able to make an appropriate response.

However, the actual adaptive responses have to be created by the individual and cannot be commanded by another.

At the beginning of a child's life, many reflexes help him or her adapt to situations. For example, when a baby is laid stomach down, the infant can lift his or her head up and turn it to breathe. Standing up in response to gravity is an adaptive response for a child of eleven or twelve months. This response is made possible by the child's newfound ability to control his or her muscles and through improved equilibrium. When the child starts to walk, movement is easier on a flat surface than on a lumpy, unpredictable floor that demands a greater adaptive response. Normal development promotes a series of successful adaptive responses. For example, with practice, a child can walk without falling, even on an uneven surface.

The Environment for SI Therapy

What does an SI therapy room look like? An SI therapy space should be visually appealing. The atmosphere is designed for the achievement of success and the enjoyment of pleasure. The space needs a certain amount of light, but the ability to lower the lighting is very helpful, especially when working with hyperactive children. The space needs to be large enough to accommodate a variety of swings, and the floor surface should be smooth enough for the child to ride a scooter board (i.e., a square wooden board low to the ground with four wheels; like a skateboard, except with wheels that rotate). It is also desirable to have a corner designated for quiet activities. The therapy space can be transformed according to each child's fantasies. For example, the child can make it into a jungle, a zoo, a desert, or an island.

The space should also contain a large selection of materials that are *sensory rich;* that is, materials with properties that are designed to promote good integration by stimulating the proprioceptive, vestibular, and tactile systems. Sensory rich does not mean having a large amount of toys, but rather a selection of sensory-appropriate toys from which the child can chose. Too many toys in one area can be overwhelming to the child.

Materials in the SI therapy space can include:

- Different sorts of swings, hammocks, tunnels, tents, large balls, and trampolines to use for movement and posture
- Whistles, blow toys, and chewing materials (e.g., bubble games and chewable tubing), which help with breath control and articulation

- Drinks and snacks to promote proper mouth movement and to help children reach the right level of alertness
- Tactile materials (e.g., putty, toys to squeeze, vibrating toys, and Koosh balls)
- Toys to look through (e.g., telescopes and pretend glasses)
- Toys that help children develop eye-hand coordination (e.g., throwing rings and balls); children also need some quiet time after using these toys, and they can cool down by using fine-motor materials (e.g., crayons and pencils) for awhile
- A scooter board with four rotating wheels

Taking some toys away after the therapy session and replacing them with other toys is one way to provide novelty. Observing whether the child cleans up and puts toys into various boxes in the therapy room is a way of learning how that child structures a space. Helping the child clean up the toys and materials is an intervention that promotes organization skills.

Play as Therapy

In normal development, play is an absolutely crucial avenue for helping children learn how their bodies work.[5] In SI therapy, play is used as well. According to Dr. Ayres, doing this effectively is part of the art and the science of SI therapy.[6]

When fun is incorporated into an activity initiated by the child, that activity can become very therapeutic. The therapist keeps in mind the goals for that child, and determines what therapeutic activity fits into the child's play at any given moment. As a result, the child always enjoys and wants to come to the therapy sessions because they are considered play.

In most SI therapy sessions the child, not the therapist, chooses the activity. When a wide variety of play materials is available, the child will choose exactly what he or she needs at that particular developmental plateau.

This sounds simple in principle, but suppose the child only wants to spin in circles. In a therapeutic situation, this would be allowed, but with modifications. The therapist would try to determine what turning in circles means to the child: Is the vestibular system not providing enough information to the brain? Is information from the muscles and joints being registering improp-

Therapy is fun!

erly? Is the child unable to stop themself despite having enough of this stimulation?

The therapist might reevaluate the child's original test results in addition to this observational data. Then, the therapist would present an intervention in the form of a game. The game would meet the spinning needs of the child, plus add an activity that is purposeful. As a result, the child would be able to respond to a higher-level task at the same time. The game might involve the child lying stomach down in a hammock spinning from one hook. The child could grab a soft ring as he or she spun around. Pushing off on the safety cushion is one way to get more proprioceptive information through the child's hands, arms, and shoulders, which involves integration and organization. The therapist also knows a child needs to stop spinning after ten times in each direction. This guidance can be built into the game so the child obtains the right amount of stimulation.

By adding a purposeful activity to the spinning (e.g., catching and throwing the ring), the therapist helps the child to become more integrated without becoming overstimulated, which could result in excessive dizziness, blanching, or redness in the face and ears. The child gets the extra benefit of back muscle development and has the chance to practice an eye-hand coordination activity, as well. Most importantly, the integrating effect of this activity generates a feeling of success. The child can say, "I did it." And the child sat-isfies his or her need to spin. This does not need to be a long activity. Some children are satisfied or feel organized after just a few minutes.

Another type of SI play that can be included in the same hour, if appropri-ate, is using a trampoline for vestibular stimulation. The child can turn in circles while jumping on the trampoline. Turning stimulates one part of the vestibular system (i.e., the semi-circular canal sensors), while jumping stimu-lates another part (i.e., the receptors in the utricles and sacculus). In addition, the child receives more information from the muscles and joints and gains greater muscular control. In this way, the child reaches a higher plateau of ac-tivity and progress than they would by just turning in circles.

Another activity that can be used when a child wants to spin involves using a sheet or a three-to-six-foot long piece of wide, flat, stretchy rubber ma-terial. The child puts this behind his or her back about waist high, faces the therapist, and gives the therapist both ends. The child runs in a circle around the therapist, while the latter turns to keep constant eye contact. In this way, the child receives a strong pressure on his or her back. Coupled with the ves-tibular input, this has a calming effect on the overactive child and helps him or her attain the integration needed to move on to another purposeful activity.

If a child has problems with a certain activity, the therapist can try to en-courage him or her to repeat an appropriate or similar developmental move-ment in a playful way. For example, the child might have a problem with rolling because his or her trunk is not stable or because rolling creates dizzi-ness as a result of repeated turning of the head. Once the therapist has identi-fied the underlying problem, the therapy can be directed to address it. The therapist might have the child simulate rolling in a play situation of the child's choosing, using heavy deep pressure to reduce the over-registration of vestibu-lar information (see Figure 5.1).

In the case of an inability to ride a bike, the therapist would seek the un-derlying reason the child cannot yet ride. The child may not be able to estab-lish balance because information from the muscles and joints is not ade-quate, he may be distracted by sounds, he may have problems processing what he or she sees, or he may be insecure about gravity and fear falling off the bike. The therapist could, for example, help the child overcome the fear of falling by discovering the pleasurable sensation of falling on a mattress. Alter-natively, the child could build a sense of balance by sitting on a ball, by using building blocks for climbing, or by sitting on a moving surface and looking at

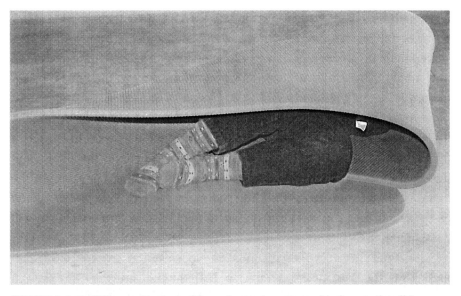

FIGURE 5.1. Rolling on a mat combines deep pressure and balance stimuli in a therapeutic activity.

a fixed focal point. As the child's problems diminish, he or she is ready to perform more complex activities in therapy and also learns to ride a bike.

If a child's development lags behind that of others of the same age, it is most helpful to find a situation in which that child can have success at his or her own level. The therapist pays close attention to the child and identifies a playful activity the child enjoys. Finding "just the right challenge" is a sign of good SI therapy.[7]

Structure Within the Treatment

A SI therapist does not always need to use a "tight" routine and structure in the therapy session. However, most therapists do have a general routine, and most hyperactive children definitely need structure in their therapy sessions. A session that has a distinct beginning, middle, and end provides clarity for the child. If the child first has to change clothes, he or she could always do so in the same way; the child's shoes, for example, should always be set down in the same spot. Likewise, the play materials can always be cleaned up and put away in the same space.

Some therapists like to start the session with a warm-up activity. Each time the child hears about warming up, he or she knows the therapist is going to do something to help that child achieve the same state of focus to prepare for a successful session. Some calming activities use deep, intense pressure, while others involve games using pulling and pushing, wrestling, or rolling over a ball. If the child can choose the warm-up activity, the child-directed therapy is off to a good start.

Many children are prepared to say what they would like to do during the therapy hour and are able to state the order in which they want to engage in the various activities. Sometimes the therapist must talk to the child about the order of activities and then summarize it for the child. For example, the therapist might summarize the child's ideas by saying, "First you are going on the swing, then you will jump on the trampoline, and your last activity will be swinging in the hammock."

The visual system is often the most developed system in hyperactive children. Thus, the child (or the therapist, or both the child and the therapist) can make a drawing of what he or she would like to happen during the session. If they discuss what will take place and then do a drawing, both the auditory and visual systems are involved. In this way, the child can learn to determine sequence and achieve control over planning a session. After every activity, the drawing of it can be checked off. For some children, it may be better if the therapist makes a drawing or summary at the end of the session.

> **TIP** **Planning**
>
> Making a list of things to be done and then checking off the items when they have been accomplished can be a useful tool in learning to be organized.

Inner Drive

One of the most important SI principles is that a child must organize his or her own thinking, based on motivation. In SI therapy, this is called *inner drive.*[8] Children should be able to express their own inner drive. Sometimes, however, the help of the therapist is needed. What the therapist says, offers, or does in therapy—in the right environment and with the right intervention— can help set the inner drive in motion.

If a child really wants to play with certain toys, that child will be highly motivated and the treatment is more likely to be effective. The child will display intense emotional involvement, excitement, and persistence while doing the task. The child has no idea that he or she is involved in a therapeutic intervention.

Naturally, some children are afraid of failing or have failed often enough or have sensory integration and motor problems. This can make it difficult for them to react positively to the therapy materials. It is a challenge for the SI-trained therapist to create an optimal situation in which the child is motivated to participate in and benefit from such an experience. To do this, the therapist must understand which activity would be most suitable for the developmental level of that child's nervous system. The situation must be tailored for each individual child. By doing this, the child can then meet the challenge and feel happy and proud of his or her success.

The Goals of Treatment

The therapist can set many different goals. One goal could be to improve the child's balance—literally and figuratively. If a hyperactive child's balance is improved, he or she will not be as distracted by falling because the child will fall less often. In general, the goal for hyperactive children is to improve the abilities of their central nervous system so that it is not overwhelmed by the amount of stimuli the child encounters. As a result, the child can attain an appropriate level of alertness.

Often hyperactive children have trouble integrating visual and auditory stimuli. As an example, consider the state of Annie when she was just beginning therapy.

ANNIE

Annie is seven years old. Her teacher is concerned about Annie's poor concentration. Annie does not sleep well, especially at the beginning of the night. She is also annoyed by the most normal stimuli at night. She has a disturbed sleep pattern and usually gets too little sleep. When she is awake, she is easily overstimulated, which is evident through her annoyance at minor details, restlessness, and mild hyperactive behavior.

When Annie wants to pay attention to something, she needs more stimuli than normal. For example, when she is trying to concentrate on reading, she needs to say the words aloud, even though she can read them perfectly well to herself under normal conditions. She cannot understand the meaning and needs many specific stimuli to be able to do the task. When she is reading a book aloud, she needs extra auditory stimuli, such as the teacher reading it together with her to help her understand what the story is about.

Annie has a great deal of difficulty concentrating and understanding schoolwork on days when her previous night's sleep was poor. The treatment goal is to help Annie find her correct arousal level so she can be calm before bedtime and be able to sleep well. A calmer level of arousal would lull her to sleep and have a naturally positive effect the next day in school. Who doesn't do better with a good night's sleep?

One goal in Annie's therapy is for her to sleep better. But she is not only a sleep-disturbed child with resulting concentration problems; she has other types of sensory dysfunctions that affect her ability to concentrate. She needs different levels of arousal or alertness for various times of the day and for various tasks. For example, when she plays softball in left field, she sometimes seems to be in a state of sleepwalking or daydreaming. This is not the correct state of alertness to catch a fly ball coming her way. To modify Annie's therapy goal, we should say that it is important for her to be able to find and profit from the correct arousal level for any situation.

A frequent goal for SI therapy is to modify the child's level of arousal. When children are overwhelmed by stimuli in their environment or by their own movement, they can be pushed to a higher arousal level. Physiological changes take place, such as increased heartbeat, perspiration, flushing, increased breathing rate, and pupil dilation. An increase in motor activity frequently occurs.

On rare occasions, children experience a different effect, a shut-down effect, from particular types of stimuli. In this situation a child's brain is somewhat like a computer that has too much information. It protects itself by not allowing more information to be taken in and processed. So in this fashion, little extra information may register. The child may look dazed or unresponsive. On very, very rare occasions, a child's breathing is affected, becoming shallow.[9] These children need an immediate change from the stimuli in the environment and need the appropriate SI therapy intervention.

In general, a child who becomes more active but who doesn't shut-down does not have the difficulties previously mentioned. When they are overstimulated, they might begin to run around or become excessively talkative. This type of child's inner motor has been jacked up to a higher speed. The word *motor*, or engine, is used in a therapeutic intervention known as "How does your engine run?" This therapy program is often used with the goal of helping children understand on a cognitive level how their "engine" is running and of teaching them strategies to help themselves arrive at a correct arousal or alertness level.[10]

TIP **Ways to Calm Down[11]**

Through taste
- Drink through a straw
- Drink a liquid that is half frozen
- Take a deep, calming breath and let the air fill up your stomach
- Eat something sweet: fruit or candy

Through the vestibular/proprioceptive system
- Play sports, play outside, and dance
- Run up and down the stairs
- Ride a bike
- Move your neck slowly in a circle, first to the right and then to the left
- Sit on a medicine ball
- Lie down or snuggle in cushions

Through touch
- Hold a toy, paper clip, rubber band, hair ornament, piece of clay, or Koosh ball
- Touch or play with a pet
- Wash your face with cold or warm water
- Take a cold, lukewarm, or hot bath

Through the visual system
- Dim the light
- Watch fish in an aquarium
- Read a book or a magazine

Through the auditory system
- Listen to classical music with a regular, soothing rhythm; Mozart often works well
- Use a headphone while listening
- Quiet your environment; turn the music off, turn the television off, speak softly or whisper

An SI Treatment Session

Suppose a child walks into the therapy space and begins the session by saying, "Today I want to climb on the ropes." By referring to the child's original evaluation information, the SI therapist knows if the child needs help in this area or if he or she can execute this activity. The therapist knows if the rope has to be adapted in any way; for example, it may need to be knotted. The therapist also knows that climbing is a very good way to increase the muscle power in hands, arms, stomach, back, and legs. It can help a child conquer the fear of having his or her feet off the ground, with no stability underneath.

Often the therapist will begin the session with some warm-up exercises. These may involve a foot and hand massage to ensure a better grip, or pushing and pulling exercises to prepare the muscles. Then the fun begins. In addition to the pleasure derived from the activity, the child gains a feeling of accomplishment. The therapist makes sure the activity is always successful and that it is safe. The therapist is empowering the child.

If the child's developmental level allows, the therapist may ask the child to make up a game while climbing the rope. The child can make up anything he or she wants. For example, the child can play at being a pirate and hang a rope to make a lookout. The pretend food for the pirate's hoard can consist of bag of small stones the child puts in his or her pocket while climbing higher. This adds weight, which strengthens the trunk, arms, and legs. Rhythmic, exciting music can be played to help build muscle tone. The child knows only that he or she is having a lot of fun. In this way, the activity stimulates the ability to fantasize, which is important for integrating the effects of SI therapy in the child's brain.

When the learning process is pleasurable, what we learn is easier to retrieve. Fun helps the memory aspects of therapy and of learning. To teach the child to be better organized, the therapist may ask questions such as "What things do we need to play pirates?" "Where should these go?" "How do you know that we have everything we need?" Through these "thinking choices," the child learns strategies that are helpful for planning and organizing.

Two or more professionals may work with the child as a team—for example, an occupational and a speech therapist, both of whom have SI training. This approach promotes a faster improvement in various areas, including language, articulation, and arousal levels.[12]

At the end of the treatment session, the therapist asks the child to say something about the activities they have done together. This strengthens the feeling of accomplishment and helps to stimulate the memory and language skills. If the child cannot yet explain what he or she did, the therapist or parent can tell the child what was done, thus strengthening the child's language comprehension abilities. If the child can say only what his or her favorite activity was, the therapist can suggest, "Perhaps next week we can play on the big swing and make another boat, as we did today." Positive emotions and anticipation are used in SI therapy to build motor and cognitive memory.

Involving Other Children

In general, SI therapy is done with one therapist and one child. Dr. Ayres developed the therapy in that way. Sometimes, however, it can help to include a second child if the child in therapy really wants to play with another child. However, the therapist must keep in mind that this is the child's special time with the therapist. So the question to be asked before bringing in another child is "Who wants to play—the friend or the child in therapy?" Usually, having a friend join the session occurs later in the course of therapy, when the child is ready for less direct intervention.

Sometimes a child wants a sibling to participate in the session. This can be supportive for certain goals, but it is not the general rule. Play therapy with a psychologist can be a valuable addition to SI therapy if it appears crucial in the early stages of treatment. If an SI therapist chooses to have another child join the therapy session, the therapist will have different goals for that session (e.g., how to play together), which will change the dynamics of the treatment session. In general, as the child's sensory integration abilities improve, his or her play skills usually improve on the playground, without other intervention, and joint play occurs as a result of the child's therapeutic changes.

Other Factors that Influence Success

Many independent factors influence the likelihood that SI therapy goals can be achieved. Returning to the example of Annie and her sleep problems that were noted at the beginning of this chapter, the therapist must consider the following factors: How seriously does Annie's behavior differ from the norm? Does the environment contribute? Are the school, the parents, and other family members involved in the treatment? Does the child faithfully attend therapy? Does the teacher use therapeutic recommendations in the classroom? Is Annie's family able to help her achieve success? Are medications being used, and if so, which ones? Do the drugs have any side effects?

Some children come for weekly sessions for a few months, and others come weekly for a year or two. Some children with greater needs may come two times a week in the beginning. Children with more complex problems (e.g., autistic spectrum disorders) often undergo therapy for a few years, and they continue to have a great time and make progress throughout that period. It is a very pleasurable experience.

Some children have a feeling about when they have obtained their optimum results from SI therapy (sometimes as early as 6 months). They may say things like things like "I want to play hockey instead of going to therapy." Other children enjoy it so much they are disappointed when the end goals are realized and they do not have to attend any longer. Then it is time for a little party emphasizing the child's accomplishment!

The Skill of the Therapist

Dr. Ayres's first book, *Sensory Integration and Learning Disabilities,* ends with a chapter entitled "The Art of Therapy." Through the years, the art and the science of SI therapy have evolved, but the therapist's respect for and understanding of the child's central nervous system remains at the core of the therapy session. A skillful SI therapist finds a friendly way to offer the child a safe space to play and have fun, while keeping SI theory and therapy goals in mind for the child's development

Training for SI Therapists: What Education Is Necessary?

SI therapists have a full undergraduate degree in one of the paramedical professions: occupational, physical, or speech therapy. They must then return to school to take additional courses. This postgraduate training may or may not lead to a certificate. Certification is coupled with being competent in SI theory, as well as being knowledgeable about diagnostic and testing techniques.

For years, Sensory Integration International (originally called the Center for the Study of Sensory Integration Dysfunction) certified therapists and provided educational services. Under Dr. Ayres, and later Patricia Oetter, it flourished as a center for study and research.

A range of other therapies coordinate well with SI and may be part of an SI therapist's training:

- Various music therapies are available. French Professors Berard and

Tomatis are two ear, nose, and throat doctors who developed an intervention using modified musical levels. Both continue to have large followings among well-trained medical staff and therapists worldwide. Therapeutic listening and sonomas are two additional approaches SI therapists can learn and incorporate with traditional SI therapy.

- Cranial sacral and myofascial release are two therapies in which the therapist takes a "hands on" approach to the patient. These mesh well with SI because the physical body of the child "tells" the therapist what to do with his or her hands on the patient's body. These therapies help release tight muscles and other fascial connections.

- Neurotherapy uses EEG-biofeedback with special software to help children learn to concentrate and focus better. On the screen, the child sees information about his or her brain activity in a way that allows the child to achieve control over it. The child learns which brain patterns go with paying attention and how to stimulate them. The child also learns which patterns go with inattentiveness and how to diminish them. Meditation works in a similar way but without the feedback.

- The metronome, an auditory and coordination exercise, is also based on biofeedback. Research has shown this to have a positive effect on handwriting and certain auditory language abilities.[13] It is obvious both neurotherapy and the metronome demand a reasonably high level of participation from the child.

SI-Trained Therapists: Where Do I Find One?

If you decide that you are interested in locating a SI-trained therapist, we have included a special listing in this book. The SI-therapy centers found in the Resource section at the end of the book provide the names of therapists in various locations. These centers can also refer you to a therapist in your area if one is not listed in this book.

Conclusions

SI treatment is an enjoyable experience that can help your child improve aspects of his or her life, at whatever age. It can help the child with play, going to school, being a family member, and being a friend. SI therapy is not only for children, but can be used with teenagers who have various learning and sensory integration problems and with people who have other neurological impairments, such as whiplash, stroke, or blindness. The therapeutic personality of a trained SI therapist gives the patient freedom to "be a child," have fun, and play, while incorporating the neurological principles mentioned in this chapter.

Chapter 6

Tips for Dealing with Your Hyperactive Child

Playing sports after school is fun.

E VERY CHILD IS UNIQUE. All children come with their own set of emotional needs and preferred ways of learning and interacting. And yet, in our SI practice, we have noticed certain ways of dealing with hyperactive children that tend to have a calming effect. We invite you to try these techniques at home and to notice which ones your child reacts to most favorably.

In addition to using the therapy techniques at home, the techniques described here can be used at school. Teachers usually need an introduction to this approach and certainly need to be open to trying a different approach in their classroom. Many of these techniques are basic techniques used frequently in special education, and it is possible that your child's teacher is already using them.

The techniques challenge your child to grow, but do so in a fun and child-friendly way. If you as a caretaker or a teacher are open to trying new ideas, we think you will find these tips have a positive effect on your child.

Communicating

The bonding between parent and child, the relationship between teacher and pupil, and even the connection between animal and child needs a good foundation before it can occur and be fruitful.[1] Sometimes with a hyperactive child, communication is disturbed because the child's attention is so flighty.

"Did he even hear what I said to him?" you might ask yourself when you see the child is already out of the room.

Consider the following suggestions:

- Look your child in the eyes before you begin speaking. If this is not possible, make sure the child is looking in your direction.

- Use the child's first name before you continue with a question or information. Do not continue until you have the child's attention.

- Touch the child to get his or her attention. Do not do this if the child has a negative reaction to touch, because you will possibly put the child in such a state of alert or flight, fight, fright, and freeze that he or she is notable to pay attention to your voice.

- If you want your child to look at something, begin the sentence with "look" and then wait awhile.

- Using the same approach, say "listen to this," "feel this," "taste this," or "smell this."

- Talk calmly and use short, easy-to-follow sentences.

- Be direct. It is easier for your child to understand you if your speech has clarity.

- Limit choices to two or three options.

- As much as possible, treat your child in a positive way. "That's great that you can do this already!" is much better than "When I was your age, I could do that already."

- React calmly but enthusiastically when a child accomplishes something. Sometimes merely saying, "Good job!" or "Great!" is enough if said in a happy voice. Remember it is the *effort* your child puts into understanding your message or performing a task that is applauded.

- Reprimands are sometimes necessary. If you must reprimand your child, do so directly and immediately. Be clear and determined. Try not to be emotional, fearful, or angry. Time-out sessions can be very short —three to as many as ten seconds works.

- Devoting fifteen minutes a day entirely to your child can accomplish wonders. If your child will curl up next to you or sit in your lap, this can be a good moment to discuss emotional issues. Your therapists may have additional ideas about using a "sensory diet" to help your child become even more organized throughout the day.

- Continue to read educational books for yourself, such as this one, that present methods of dealing with hyperactive children.

Organizing the Day

Determine if you can organize your day around the following points:

- If possible, organize the day in a way the child finds easy to accept.

- Get up early to avoid rushing in the morning.

- Build a few quiet periods into every day, both for yourself and your child.

- Every now and then, make time to be alone with your child; for example, go for a walk with the child instead of with the whole family.

- Structure does not always have to do with time, but rather with a determined order of things and events. This can change from day to day, but your child can count on generally knowing how the day will proceed before it starts. However, too much structure can make a child rigid and imprison a family. Try to find the structure that fits your family.

Fostering Calmness

As you work with your child, train yourself to radiate calmness. In order to cultivate a calm and alert attitude, you may find it helpful to take up a sport or practice yoga, tai chi, or qigong. Or express yourself through a hobby.

You may be able to calm your child in the following ways:

- Identify your own emotional state and attend to it, as necessary.

- Give the child a short (i.e., ten second) time-out. This is not punishment, but rather a moment that allows the child to get himself or herself together. It would also be helpful for you and your child to do deep breathing during this time.

- Lower your voice (i.e., speak softly but audibly) and breathe slowly even though the atmosphere has become chaotic. Your child will automatically breathe along in the slower tempo and become calmer.

- Your young child will become calmer if you hold his or her hand firmly in a friendly way. It can also help if your child is holding something in the other hand (e.g., a teddy bear or a ball).

- Place your hand on your child's shoulder or another acceptable place. Gently holding it in one position can promote a restful feeling.

- Let your child push his or her hands together and apply strong pressure on the palms.

- If your child is really restless, try giving him or her a strong, calm hug; place both arms around your child and hold him or her firmly against you.

- Use your hands to apply firm pressure on your child's shoulders or apply a series of ten short pushes downward on the shoulders.

- If possible, make the environment as quiet as possible. Turn off any loud music or play quiet classical music. Many children find listening to Mozart very relaxing. Turn the TV off or turn the volume down. Busy, hectic images can agitate your child, so look for soothing images.

- Rock your child slowly on your lap, in a hammock, or on a swing.

These last two are good for people of any age:

- Lying in a position in which the head is lower than the heart can lower blood pressure and help your child become calmer. To do this, a small child can lie stomach down over your knees, with their head hanging downward, while you sit on a sofa. Bigger children can hang over the sofa or over a swing outside. You may have noticed children sometimes seek out this position themselves for a short calming period.

- Wash your child slowly in warm water.

- Give your child a warm bath before going to school.

- Calmly rub the length of your child's forehead or let your child rub it.

- Slowly massage your child's back, legs, and arms with a firm but gentle pressure.

- Massage the soles of your child's feet.

- Make it possible for your child to move if he or she has been sitting still for a long time. Give your child a chore to do—such as watering the plants or getting something for you (the more physical the job is, the better, within reason, of course)—or have your child run back and forth outside for a few minutes, just as a calming down technique.

- Use calming scents, such as lavender and vanilla.

- Watch out for food additives to which your child may be oversensitive. Food dyes, chemical smells, taste enhancers, sugar, and other ingredients can provoke oversensitivity that causes bad behavior. Seek expert advice to find out to which foods or additives your child may be oversensitive.

- Drinking a soft drink through a straw can calm your child.

- Allow your child to cool off by sucking or chewing on a piece of ice. An ice cube made with juice is appealing.

Giving Directions

Give directions in a structured way:

- Make sure the environment is calm. Pay attention to the multitude of sounds, colors, brightness, and other factors in the environment that might stimulate or overstimulate your child. If necessary, go to another room before you give your child a command.

- Breathe slowly.

- Move and react calmly, speak softly, and lower your voice. Use few words.

- Break chore assignments into smaller assignments and give one order at a time. Be sure the first part of the order has been carried out before you introduce the next one.

- React to the chores your child has carried out as you wished them to be done. Do this in a pleasant, positive way: "Thank you for getting your shoes on so quickly. Good job." Remember that when the orders are not carried out according to your wishes, it is better not to respond. Instead, next time you make the same assignment, think of a better way to structure it so your child can more easily accomplish it. This means success for your child, and you can give praise for a job well done.

Avoiding Injury

The following measures can help prevent injuries:

- Make sure your child wears a bicycle helmet. Find the safest bicycle routes.

- As often as necessary, remind your child to use safety precautions and avoid risky activities. Step in, if necessary, to assure this.

- Be vigilant if your child is involved in risky activities, such as swimming, climbing, going on amusement park rides, or going to a large indoor gym.

- Keep dangerous products and tools out of the hands of your young child.

- Young adults with ADHD have to be extra careful when driving. They can listen to soft music, but, of course, they should not use alcohol or drugs. They should not use a cell phone or headphones when driving. Preferably, no other passengers should be in the car; if someone else must be in the car, make sure that person will act appropriately. In advance of any trip, plan the route carefully with your teenager.

Making Necessary Adaptations

Therapists with SI training make adaptations for the symptoms of hyperactive children. You can also make these types of adaptations at home, at school, and while children are playing. For example, if your child becomes overwrought in a room full of toys, it is a good idea to modify the situation. Providing well-marked boxes in which your child can put the toys gives him or her a sense of control. Adaptation can be particularly important for a birthday party or similar situation. For example, inviting fewer friends and featuring fewer activities can make the event more fun for your hyperactive child. Adaptations to the home, play setting, and other environments are among the most effective interventions a family can provide while the child is becoming more integrated. Later, these preventive measures can be lessened as your child changes and learns to handle many situations.

Toys

Let your child play with or on large toys, such as cushions, blankets, and a trampoline. The child has to be able to be creative in play. Preferably, involve him or her in a physical game. You can hang a large board on the wall on which your child can draw. Do not make the play space too busy, use battery-operated toys as little as possible, and avoid toys that make noise. Limit time spent playing with a Game Boy or computer and watching television. Let your child play outside before and after watching TV. Maintain these limits consistently.

Let your child play with building toys (e.g., Lego, Knex, and Duplo) on the carpet, not on a table. Establish firm rules. For example, have your child put the pieces in their box when he or she is finished playing with them; do not allow throwing. As often as possible, take your child to the playground or to the woods. In general, children are calmer outdoors.

Sports

Hyperactive children can benefit from sports. After a sports activity, your child will be more organized and less hyperactive for a while. In principle, any sport is suitable *if* your child is interested in it. Care should be taken not to force a child to participate in a sport. Children with tactile aversion or defensiveness may feel threatened and uncomfortable. As SI therapy progresses, these reactions will change and the child usually becomes more ready for participation.

A few sports are particularly therapeutic: The first is horseback riding. This sport is excellent because it involves interaction with an animal, which your child can find magical. And, of course, riding provides vestibular stimuli—both through the soothing action of the rocking motion and through the acceleration of movement. Riding is a good way to improve muscle tone through the slight bouncing that occurs. In this way, balance is naturally challenged and improved.

Judo and other martial arts sports are also very well suited because of their discipline and physical aspect, which involves applying deep pressure. Although these sports may not be suited for children who are oversensitive to certain tactile stimuli or unexpected movement, some children occasionally crave deep pressure. Check that the instructor or teacher understands and respects your child's needs.

Soccer is well suited for hyperactive children because it involves continual running back and forth. As a team sport, it has the advantage of engaging your child as part of a group.

Swimming is a good sport, but if your child only plays around in the pool, he or she can feel overwhelmed and become more rather than less hyperactive as a result. The noisy atmosphere of an indoor pool can be even more distressing than an outside pool. All organized swimming activities require supervision for safety and to reduce the risk of your child becoming too overwhelmed by all the sensations. If this happens, give your child a break or switch to a less stimulating location.

Children with tactile processing problems sometimes need help before they get into the water. Some children with tactile aversion have trouble with the little sprinkles in the showering procedures prior to swimming. Your SI therapist can problem solve with your child and the swimming instructor to adapt the sensory situation into an acceptable procedure rather than a distressing one.

TIP Negotiating the Classroom

In the classroom, pay attention to the following:

- If your child moves around a lot, he or she may be better off sitting on a moveable chair, on a cushion, or on a large ball. This promotes good extension in the back and helps your child become more stable and thus less wiggly in general.

- Chewing gum can help your child concentrate on his or her work. Gum stimulates different parts of the brain in a helpful manner. (This is not an intervention that all schools will embrace, so check before sending your child to school with gum.)

- Your child may be calmer if he or she sits near the teacher or near a child who is calm.

- If your child has tactile processing problems, he or she needs to be able to see the other children in the class. In this case, your child will usually work best at a seat in the back or on the side of the room, a little distance from other children. In this way, your child can keep an eye on the situation and not feel so threatened and, thus, be better able to attend to the class work.

Minimizing Tactile Defensiveness

The sensory problem of tactile defensiveness or aversion deserves extra attention here because Dr. Ayres originally connected this type of behavior with hyperactivity. The other sensory systems can certainly be overwhelmed and lead to attention and concentration problems, as well.

If your child has tactile processing problems, you can try the following at home:

- When you touch your child, use strong pressure.
- Tickling, pinching, and touching lightly with the fingertips should

generally be avoided because these types of touch can be perceived by your child as painful and threatening.

However, many parents tell us their children like being gently touched or slightly tickled on the back. This is the case even though these same children have tactile problems in various other situations. So, remember that there can be appropriate times for various types of touch, provided your child responds positively. Sometimes certain tickling and laughing behavior makes it look like the child is having fun, but these responses can be a nervous or negative reaction to this tickling. It might be appropriate to discuss your situation with your therapist. Even though a certain touching style is your habit, another might be even more beneficial.

- Warn your child if you are going to touch him or her.
- Without even realizing it, your child may feel very threatened when someone leans against or kisses him or her. Respect the space your child feels he or she needs.
- You can warn family and friends who might want to kiss your child that he or she does not like it and let them know you would appreciate if they did not put the child into a position to reject or even hit them.
- In the case of an unexpected touch, your child may react strongly. Expressing your understanding shows you respect his or her way of processing information. You do not need to exaggerate your own response.
- After a bath, let your child dry themself with a rough hand towel, rubbing firmly.
- If hair washing is a problem, let your child do it by themself. Give your child a washcloth to hold over the eyes or on the forehead. If you must wash your child's hair, let your child look into an unbreakable mirror while you do it. This gives him a chance to have advanced warning about what will happen. This "control" can be very reassuring.
- Make sure many different materials are present in your child's environment with which he or she can play, and thus learn to deal with touch stimuli. You may want to place a lambskin rug or a thick towel on the floor by your child's bed.
- Let your child play with bubble wrap, beads, stickers, clay, and sand. You can put some materials (e.g., clay, liquid soap, talcum powder,

freeze-dried coffee) in plastic sandwich bags. Make sure they are very securely tied before giving them to your child. Balloons can also be partially filled. You can offer these items to your child to squeeze and play with, but do not insist if your child is not interested at first. Just put the item down and begin playing with it yourself. Every now and then, ask your child to join in. The child has to want to do so in order to find it fun.

Chapter 7

Scientific Insight

We prefer our therapy to be evidence based.

M
ANY SCIENTISTS ARE actively seeking insight into subjects such as ADD and ADHD. Within SI therapy, much research has been already been undertaken and published. Lynn Horowitz's first publication of research conducted at the Amsterdam Medical Center, in the Netherlands, described the positive effects associated with six months of SI therapy. She measured the fluidity of eye movements and the time the child required to organize eye movements.[1] Dr. Ayres specifically asked Ms. Horowitz to publish this research.

Furthermore, Lynn Horowitz conducted extensive research in conjunction with consultation bureaus in the towns of Heemstede and Lelystad, also in the Netherlands. That study evaluated the sensory functions of 175 babies, from four to eighteen months of age. The results were presented at a conference in London.[2] She and Dr. W. R. A. Duurkoop are currently analyzing the results of a large study concerning children's motor skills, called "Motor Observations," for children five to twelve years of age. This is a modification of Dr. A. J. Ayres's "Clinical Observations," presented in London.[3]

With today's Internet capabilities, it is easier to stay informed about the latest research results. When you read material at such sites, be sure to remain critical. To understand the full value of the research, you have to read the entire article. Do not assume the conclusions are correct, and remember that not all conclusions can be generalized.

Examples of recently published research include the following:

- Azrin, Nathan H., Christopher T. Ehle, and Amy L. Beaumont. "Physical Exercise as a Reinforcer to Promote Calmness of an ADHD Child." *Behavioral Modification* 30, no. 5 (September 2006): 564–570.

  This study of a four-year-old boy with ADHD found that attentive calmness was substantially increased by using a period of physical activity as a reinforcer for attentive calmness. The results suggested the usefulness of a physical activity as an addition or substitute for the usual reinforcers in contingency management (behavior modification) with ADHD children.

- Barkley, R. A., M. Fischer, L. Smallish, and K. Fletcher. "Young Adult Follow-Up of Hyperactive Children: Antisocial Activities and Drug Use." *Journal of Child Psychology and Psychiatry and Allied Disciplines* 45 no. 2 (February 2004): 195–211.

  It is often said that hyperactive children (especially those with behavior problems) have a higher risk of developing antisocial behavior and experimenting with drugs when they become teens or young adults than do children who are not hyperactive. In this research, the self-reported data of twenty- and twenty-one-year-olds were analyzed. Parents were asked about medication use and hyperactivity in their children. Information about 147 young adults with earlier hyperactivity and 73 young adults without earlier incidence of hyperactivity were compared. The result showed that the hyperactive group had a higher incidence of theft and had many other forms of antisocial behavior than did the control group. ADHD in children, teens, and adults predicted a greater amount of drug-related activity. Also, behavioral problems predicted a greater amount and degree of drug-related activity with more variety in patterns of use.

- Bilic, M., F. Yilidrim, S. Kandil, M. Bekaroglu, S. Yildirmis, O. Deger, M. Ulgen, A. Yildiran, and H. Aksu. "Double-Blind, Placebo-Controlled Study of Zinc Sulfate in the Treatment of Attention Deficit Hyperactivity Disorder." *Neuropharmacology and Biological Psychiatry* 28, no. 1 (January 2003): 181–190.

  Not all patients react well to the psycho-stimulant medications that are often prescribed. As a result, there is much interest in alternative, non-stimulant therapies. A few studies have suggested that zinc deficiency could play an important role in the emergence of ADHD. This double-blind study separated a group of 400 children with a DSM-IV diagnosis of ADHD into two groups. The children were an average of 9.6 years old. One group received 150 mg zinc sulfate for twelve weeks and the other received a placebo for twelve weeks. Extensive evaluations were conducted with the help of a recognized ADHD questionnaire for parents and teachers.

The results showed that zinc sulfate had a more positive influence on hyperactivity, impulsivity, and general behavior in school than did the placebo. This was the case with older children who had low levels of zinc and monounsaturated fatty acids. Concentration problems were not reduced. Zinc sulfate was well tolerated and there were few side effects.

Brazelton, T. Berry. "ADHD Children Have Different Symptoms." *Contra Costa Times*, April 23, 2003.

The well-known pediatrician T. Berry Brazelton explains how other behavioral problems can seem like ADHD. This is especially true for children with a subtype of ADHD in which inattention is the primary symptom. This article explains, in layman's terms, which symptoms parents should look for that might be related to such conditions as anxiety, depression, giftedness, hearing problems, or learning disorders, and not to ADHD.

Chervin, Ronald, K. Archbold, J. Dillon, P. Panahi, K. Pituch, R. Dahl, and C. Guilleminault. "Inattention, Hyperactivity and Symptoms of Sleep Disordered Breathing." *Pediatrics* 109, no. 3 (March 2002): 449–456.

The results of this research conclude that certain types of inattention and hyperactivity are related to sleep disordered breathing. This is also associated with daytime sleepiness and snoring, especially in young boys. The results suggest this could have a major health impact. Other researchers have mentioned that medicine for sleep problems may be able to help alleviate hyperactivity symptoms.

Christakis, D. A., F. J. Zimmerman, D. L. DiGiuseppe, and C. A. McCarty. "Early Television Exposure and Subsequent Attention Problems in Children." *Pediatrics* 113, no. 4 (April 2004): 708–713.

Children who start to watch television at a young age may have a higher risk of developing inattention. As part of a long-term study,

D. A. Christakis, the father of two young children, investigated this aspect. He noticed how enthusiastic his three-month-old baby was about the television. His study involved two age groups: 1,278 children who were one year old and 1,345 children who were three years old. The parents kept a tally of the amount of time their children watched television. When the children were seven years old, another questionnaire was administered regarding behavioral factors. The results showed that a three-year-old child who watched two hours of television each day had a higher risk of having problems with attention at the age of seven than did a three-year-old who never watched television. One possible explanation is that images on television alternate faster than they do in real life. The author asked if the development of language would be delayed for a child who only watched television because no one else repeated and confirmed the words. The American Academy of Pediatrics cautioned parents to be careful about letting children younger than two years old watch television.

■ Chronis, A. M., B. B. Lahey, W. E. Pelham Jr., H. L. Kipp, B. L. Baumann, and S. S. Lee. "Psychopathology and Substance Abuse in Parents of Young Children with Attention Deficit/Hyperactivity Disorder." *Journal of the American Academy of Child and Adolescent Psychiatry* 42, no. 12 (December 2003): 1424–1432.

More than twenty articles confirmed that ADHD has a genetic factor, according to a review of research conducted by these researchers. Parents, nieces, and nephews can display symptoms of ADHD. Chronis and colleagues found that parents of children with ADHD—in this case the mothers—were twenty-four times more likely to have ADHD than were parents of children who did not have ADHD. If the child had received a diagnosis of oppositional defiant disorder behavioral problems, the chance that the parents had mood disorders, anxiety, addictions, and depression was increased, as well. According to research, one in twenty American parents has ADHD, of which only fifteen to twenty-five percent are conscious of the disorder. This research recommended that treatment should not just include the children, but should offer guidance for other family problems.

■ DiScala, Carla, Ilana Leschohier, Martha Barthel, and Guohua Li. "Injuries to Children with Attention Deficit Hyperactivity Disorder." *Pediatrics* 102, no. 6 (December 1998): 1415–1421.

As pedestrians and when riding on bicycles, children with ADHD were more often hurt than were their non-ADHD peers. They had more frequent head injuries, injuries to more parts of their bodies, and injuries that did more lasting damage. In addition, they had more frequent hospital admissions due to poisonous substance intake.

- Durston, Sarah. "Imaging Brain Structure and Function in Attention Deficit Hyperactivity Disorder." Doctoral thesis at UMC Utrecht: Ponsen & Looijen BV, Wageningen, Netherlands, January 2003.

Magnetic resonance imaging (MRI) of boys with ADHD showed certain anatomic areas of the brain to be smaller than in boys without ADHD. In the brothers of these children, the difference was also noticeable. However, the brothers did not have this anatomical disparity in the cerebellum, although they were presumed to have a higher genetic risk of ADHD. Children with ADHD used a more diffuse network in various areas of their brains used for conscious control than did children without ADHD. The study concluded that there may be different types of ADHD, or subtypes with specific, subtle variations in brain anatomy.

- Klingberg, T., H. Forssberg, and H. Westerberg. "Training of Working Memory in Children with ADHD." *Journal of Clinical Experimental Neuropsychology* 24, no. 6 (September 2002): 781–791.

Working memory is the ability to keep and process information for a short period of time. This ability is generally considered to be something every individual possesses. This double-blind research showed that training the working memory can improve it. This specific training also seemed to improve spatial perception and to reduce extra head movements. A second experiment showed these techniques could improve the cognitive tasks of young adults without ADHD.

- Teicher, Martin. "Actigraphy and Motion Analysis: New Tools for Psychiatry." *Harvard Review of Psychiatry* 3, no. 1 (1995): 18–35.

The author updated this research in 2002–2003 with a study entitled "Using Infrared Analysis of Movement and Measuring Electronic Activity to Diagnose ADHD and Other Problems" (personal communication). This study found that it is possible to distinguish children with ADHD, posttraumatic stress, or depression from other children without psychiatric problems by using infrared movement analysis and by measuring electronic activity. This discovery promises more precise

119

diagnoses and may point toward the discovery of biological changes associated with behavioral problems. An important area of the brain under investigation is the vermis, the median part of the cerebellum.

■ Well, Karen C., Terry C. Chi, Stephen P. Hinshaw, Jeffery N. Epstein, Linda Pfiffner, Marie Nebel-Schwalm, Elizabeth B. Owens, L. Eugene Arnold, Howard B. Abikoff, C. Keith Conners, Glen R. Elliott, Laurence L. Greenhill, Lily Hechtman, Betsy Hoza, Peter S. Jensen, John March, Jeffrey H. Newcorn, William E. Pelham, Joanne B. Severe, James Swanson, Benedetto Vitiello, and Timothy Wigal. "Treatment Related Changes in Objectively Measured Parenting Behaviors in the Multimodal Treatment Study of Children with Attention-Deficit/Hyperactivity Disorder." *Journal of Consulting and Clinical Psychology* 74, no. 4 (August 2006): 649–657.

This study was organized through Duke University's Department of Psychiatry. It evaluated the outcome of a multimodel study involving 579 ethnically and socio-economically diverse children with ADHD (ages 7.0 to 9.9 years) and their parents. The subjects were recruited from six sites in the United States and Canada. They were randomly assigned to one of four groups for intervention: medicine, behavior therapy, a combination of medication and behavior therapy, and a control group attending community treatment. Observers who were blind to the treatment conditions evaluated the parents. The behavior of the children whose parents received help with behavioral strategies and their children who received medication improved significantly. However, the effect of only one treatment on child behavior or on parental support was not significant. The authors discuss the importance of changing parenting behaviors.

Chapter 8

A Questionnaire for Parents

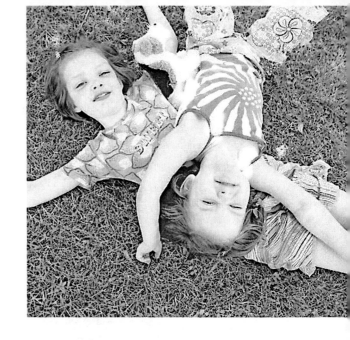

Does my child have sensory integration problems?

T HE "TEN QUICK QUESTION" checklist from *Sensational Kids* by Lucy Jane Miller gives parents a way to determine if a sensory processing problem is occurring in their children.[1] It is not specifically geared for a child with hyperactivity, but it can be very useful because many problems overlap.

Ten Quick Questions

Families of sensational kids typically respond yes to two or more of the following statements. Checklists with the specific symptoms of Sensory Processing Disorder and its subtypes can be found in Part I of Sensational Kids.

- ❑ My child has seemed "different" from other children almost from birth, but our doctor cannot tell me why.

- ❑ My child feels "different" from other kids and tends to isolate himself or herself from them.

- ❑ My child seems "behind" in development even though no medical or developmental condition has been identified that would cause a delay.

❑ Teachers say my child doesn't respond like the other students in classroom and playground situations.

❑ I've noticed that my child doesn't respond to some sensations (touch, sound, smell, taste, movement, or others) the way the rest of the family or other children the same age do.

❑ My neighbor/friend/relative who has a child with Sensory Processing Disorder told me I ought to have my child screened for the condition.

❑ When I read the "Red Flags" for Sensory Processing Disorder in Sensational Kids, I recognized my child's behavior in at least one of the subtypes.

❑ My child has screened positive for sensory issues at a kindergarten round-up, well-child visit, or in another evaluative situation.

❑ I feel something's "wrong" with my child, but I don't know what it is.

❑ My child feels like something's "wrong" with him/her, and that's causing low self-confidence and self-esteem.

A more extensive SI questionnaire was developed by Cecile Röst in Leiden, the Netherlands, to identify sensory integration problems in general. Röst's work is based on many previous SI diagnostic questionnaires.[2] We have included this questionnaire to show you with which areas SI therapists are concerned. If you wish, you may consult a trained SI therapist, who can evaluate your answers to determine if therapy is the next move. The therapist may want your child's teacher to fill out a separate questionnaire especially developed to evaluate SI problems in the school setting. This school questionnaire is usually given by the therapist to the parent, who then asks the teacher to fill it out.

General Information

Name of your child: _____

Birth date: _____

Address: _____

City, State, Zip: _____

Telephone: _____ Cell phone: _____

E-mail: _____

Name of school: _____

Telephone: _____

Name of teacher: _____

Grade: _____

Pediatrician: _____

Telephone: _____

Referring physician: _____

Other specialists: _____

_____

_____

Ages of brothers and sisters: _____

Pregnancy and Delivery

Age of the mother when the child was born: _____

How long did the pregnancy last? _____ weeks

How did the pregnancy proceed? _____

How did the delivery go? _____

What was the child's birth weight? _____ lbs., _____ oz.

Was your child blue?   YES   NO

Did your child require oxygen?   YES   NO

Was your baby placed in a neonatal intensive care unit?   YES   NO

Do you know your child's Apgar score?   0–5   6–8   9–10

Were there feeding problems?   YES   NO   If yes, provide details:

_____

_____

Were there sleeping problems?   YES   NO   If yes, provide details:

_____

_____

School Information

Did your child attend other schools before his current school?   YES   NO

If so, why did he or she change schools?

_____

_____

_____

Did your child skip a school year/repeat a year?   YES / NO

Has your child attended a special educational program in or outside of
school?   YES / NO

Were there problems in daycare/nursery school?   YES / NO

Please circle what is appropriate:

Did the child have difficulty with:

finger painting	sandbox play	drawing
cutting	puzzles	fastening buttons
gymnastics	stringing beads	tying shoelaces
projects requiring the use of glue		

Has your child had trouble:

using a pen or pencil	cutting things out	doing jigsaw puzzles
making pottery	doing embroidery	writing
reading	using language	doing math
doing gymnastics	doing chores	
using construction materials (such as Lego)		

Explanation: _____

_____

_____

Illnesses and Hospital Admissions

	Yes	No	Comments
Is your child often sick?			
If so, what conditions does your child display?			
Does your child have allergies? If so, to what is he or she allergic?			
Does your child have ear problems?			
Does your child get headaches?			
Does your child have eye problems?			
Does your child have a problem with dizziness?			
Has your child ever had an epileptic seizure? If so, was it a petit mal, a small blackout, or a short loss of attention?			
Are there other complaints?			
Has your child ever been admitted to the hospital? If so, what for?			
Has your child ever had a CT-scan, an MRI scan, an EEG, X rays? If so, which ones and why?			
Has your child taken psychological or other diagnostic tests? If so, which tests were taken and what were the results?			
Has your child received therapy? If so, what kind of therapy and with what goals and results?			
When and how often did the therapy take place?			

Development

Please fill in how old your child was when he or she was first able to accomplish certain tasks. If you do not know exactly, but there was nothing unusual about the development, write "normal" in the "age" column. Write "not yet" if your child has not yet accomplished the activity.

	Age
Touch	
Plays with hands	
Plays with feet	
Explores things with mouth	
Explores things with hands	
Communication	
First laugh	
First words	
First two-word sentence	
Motor Skills	
Rolls over	
Sitting	
Crawling	
Standing	
Walking	
Bicycling on a three-wheeler	
Bicycling on a bicycle without side wheels	
Swimming	
Daily Activities	
Drinks from a cup	
Eats with a spoon	
Stays dry day and night	
Undresses himself	
Dresses herself	
Fastens buttons and closes zippers	
Ties laces	

Behaviors

Are the following assertions applicable to your child? (You can add more details on a separate sheet of paper; these can be helpful.)

	True	False
Touch		
While eating, the child often turns his or her face to the side, seeming to avoid the spoon.		
The child finds it irritating to be held close.		
The child does not like to be washed.		
Balance		
The child stiffens if he or she is picked up.		
The child looks anxious when sitting on the toilet.		
The child only calms down when walking or riding in the car.		
The child cries frequently while walking.		
The child does not like to be rocked.		
The child does not enjoy being tossed into the air.		
Oral Skills		
Sucking was poor during bottle/breast feeding.		
Swallowing cereal or other solid food is difficult.		
Chewing food is difficult.		
The child cannot blow out a candle well.		
Emotional/Social Behavior		
The child cries a lot.		
The child was a very busy baby.		
The child is very timid.		
The child almost never wants to play alone.		
The child cannot play well with other children.		

Current Behaviors

The child is: left-handed _____ right-handed _____

Fill in the following chart sections based on how your child has been behaving recently.

	True	False
Motor Skills		
Ungainly		
Unhandy		
Slow		
Stumbles often		
Often walks or bumps into things		
Movements are often too hard or too soft		
Often walks on his or her toes		
Often sits in a crooked position, slouches, or slumps over		
Touch		
Avoids playing with dirty things, such as mud or clay		
Does not like sandboxes or the beach		
Does not like people to touch him or her unexpectedly		
Does not like to be hugged		
Jumps off if he or she is sitting on someone's lap		
Only likes to be touched if he or she takes the initiative		
Has an aversion to certain clothing material		
Does not like to have his or her face washed or cleaned		
Hates getting a haircut		
Hates having his or her nails cut		
Hits himself or herself on purpose		
Seems to experience less pain than other children do		
Seems to experience more pain than other children do		

	True	False
Balance		
Afraid of heights		
Little interest in climbing		
Never sees danger while playing		
Cannot handle the sensation of making turns on playground equipment and avoids this type of motion		
Does not like swings		
Turns or swings a great deal		
Avoids games that involve balance		
Does not fall well; frequently skins knees or injures self		
Likes to fall and does so often		
Avoids falling		
Feels afraid in a large, open space		
Frequently or quickly becomes carsick		
Communication, Language, and Speech		
Difficult to understand because of poor articulation		
Speaks noticeably little		
Uses gestures in place of using difficult words		
Instead of naming things, often points to them		
Pulls on people to express his or her wishes		
Substitutes easy words (e.g., "this" and "that") instead of using the appropriate word		
Speaks haltingly		
Cannot pronounce some sounds correctly		
Tells a story in an illogical way		
Has difficulty relating a life experience		
Has difficulty understanding instructions		
Has difficulty carrying out a chore		

(cont'd.)

Current Behaviors (cont'd.)

	True	False
Hearing and Seeing		
Reacts to an unexpected sound in a negative way		
Reacts strangely to loud noises		
Often screams or speaks shrilly		
Often holds his or her hands over the ears in response to loud noises (e.g., fire trucks)		
Gets distracted by sounds		
Wears glasses		
Has difficulty following an object with his or her eyes		
Often loses his or her place in the text while reading or writing		
Gets distracted by what he or she sees		
Emotional/Social Behavior		
Oversensitive to criticism		
Afraid to fail		
Withdrawn		
Difficulty adapting to changes or unexpected situations		
Manipulates the environment		
Quickly irritated		
Quick to anger		
A perfectionist		
Disorganized, chaotic		
Contact with others is difficult		
Is teased by others		
Has difficulty playing with others; often plays alone		
Often fights with other children		
Disturbs other children		
Prefers to play with children who are much younger		
Prefers to play with children who are much older		

	True	False
Is always moving, extremely active		
Is always wobbling, wriggling, or rubbing		
Attention		
Is easily distracted		
Does not listen carefully to a story		
Cannot follow a television story		
Restless		
Often lost in thought		
Does not listen to what you say		
Cannot sit still		

What do you think is the most important area that needs attention for your child?

_____

_____

_____

Endnotes

Preface

1. Lynn Horowitz, Ank Verschoor, Maria Wessels, Regien Hogerheijde, Anita Ooster-
baan, Annete Scheper, Eelke van Haeften, and Saskia Vriesinga, *Een Behandeling voor
Stoornissen in de Sensorische Ingtegatie* [A Therapy for Disorders in Sensory Integra-
tion] (Santpoort-Zuid, Netherlands: Sensory Integration Services and Research,
2002).

Chapter 1

1. Barbara M. Knickerbocker, *A Holistic Approach to the Treatment of Learning Disorders*
(Thorofare, NJ: Charles B. Slack, 1980).
2. Patricia A. Oetter, "Assessment: The Child with Attention Deficit Disorders," *Sensory
Integration Special Interest Section Newsletter* 9 (1986): 1.
3. Maryann Colby Trott, Marci K. Laurel, and Susan L. Windeck, *Sense Abilities: Understanding Sensory Integration* (Tucson, AZ: Psych Corp. 1993).
4. A. Jean Ayres, *Sensory Integration and the Child* (Los Angeles: Western Psychological
Services, 1980).
5. A. Jean Ayres, *Sensory Integration and Learning Disorders* (Los Angeles: Western Psychological Services, 1972).
6. ibid.
7. A. Jean Ayres, *Southern California Sensory Integration Tests* (Los Angeles, CA: Western
Psychological Services, 1972).
8. A. Jean Ayres, *Sensory Integration and Learning Disorders.*
9. Lucy Jane Miller, *Sensational Kids* (Penguin, New York: 2006).
10. Patricia Wilbarger and Julie Wilbarger, *Sensory Defensiveness in Children 2 Years to 12*
(Stillmore, MN: PDP Press, Inc, 1995).
11. George J. DuPaul and Gary Stoner, *ADHD in the Schools* (New York: Guilford Press,
1994).
12. Barbara M. Knickerbocker, *A Holistic Approach to the Treatment of Learning Disorders.*
13. A. Jean Ayres, *Sensory Integration and Praxis Test* (Los Angeles: Western Psychological Services, 1989).

14. Liesbeth Collard and Nederlandse Centrum voor Sensorische Integratie, *Cursus Manual Deel I-Hyperactivity* (Rotterdam, Netherlands: Haarlem/Transfer Groep, 2006).

15. Judith G. Kimball, "Case History Follow-up Report," *Center for the Study of Sensory Integrative Dysfunction Newsletter* (1977), 1–3.

16. Judith G. Kimball, "Prediction of Methylphenidate (Ritalin) Responsiveness Through Sensory Integrative Testing," *American Journal of Occupational Therapy* 40 (1986): 241–248.

17. Winifred Dunn and C. Brown, "Factor Analysis on the Sensory Profile from a National Sample of Children without Disabilities," *American Journal of Occupational Therapy* 51, no. 17 (1997): 490–495.

18. Winifred Dunn, "Sensory Profile Training Course Worksheet for Analysis of Visual/Tactile Processing Cluster Related to Children with ADHD," *SINETwork* 41 (2002): 27–29.

Chapter 2

1. Anne G. Fisher, Elizabeth A. Murray, and Anita C. Bundy, *Sensory Integration Theory and Practice* (Philadelphia, PA: Davis, 1991).

2. George J. DuPaul and Gary Stoner, *ADHD in the Schools.*

3. Sensory Integration International, Workgroup on ADHD and SI, "Characteristics and Temperament of ADHD and SI Children," *Sensory Integration Quarterly* (1996).

4. Carol Stock Kranowitz, *Out of Sync Child* (New York: Berkley, 1998).

5. C. K. Conners, "Food Additives and Hyperkinesis: A Controlled Double-Blind Experiment," *Pediatrics* 58, no. 2 (1976): 154–166.

6. Lydia M. J. Pelsser, "De Invloed van Voeding op Hyperactief Gedrag, Gemeten bij Kinderen die Voldoen aan de Criteria voor ADHD" [The effect of food on hyperactive behavior as measured in children meeting the ADHD criteria], *Kind en Adolescent* (2002) 146; 2543–2547.

7. Lydia M. J. Pelsser, "De Invloed van Voeding op Hyperactief Gedragbij Kinderen met ADHD" [The effect of food on hyperactive behavior in children with ADHD], *Kind en Adolescent* (2003): 4–16.

8. Patricia Wilbarger and Patricia A. Oetter, "A Sensory Diet and Use of a Deep Pressure for Sensory Defensiveness," Sensory Defensiveness Symposium in Haarlem, Netherlands: Netherlands Center for Sensory Integration, 1995.

9. Carol Stock Kranowitz, *Out of Sync Child.*

10. D. M. Ross and S. A. Ross, *Hyperactivity: Current Issues, Research and Theory,* 2nd ed. (New York: Wiley, 1982).

11. Maryann Colby Trott, Marci K. Laurel, and Susan L. Windeck, *Sense Abilities,* 1993.

12. A. Jean Ayres, *Sensory Integration and the Child* (Los Angeles, CA: Western Psychological Services, 1980).

13. Patricia Wilbarger and Patricia A. Oetter, "A Sensory Diet and Use of a Deep Pressure for Sensory Defensiveness."

Chapter 3

1. Patricia Wilbarger and Julie Wilbarger, *Sensory Defensiveness in Children 2 Years to 12* (Stillmore, MN: PDP Press, Inc, 1995).
2. Patricia A. Oetter, "Sensory Integrative Approach to the Treatment of Attention Deficit Disorders," *Sensory Integration Special Interest Section Newsletter* 9 (1986): 2.
3. Joy Huss of Cerebral Palsy Center/Indiana University Medical Center, Indianapolis, IN, personal communication, 1969.

Chapter 4

1. Susan A. Greenfield, *The Human Mind Explained* (New York: Henry Holt, 1996).
2. Patricia Wilbarger and Julie Wilbarger, *Sensory Defensiveness in Children 2 Years to 12* (Stillmore, MN: PDP Press, Inc, 1995).
3. Bernadette van Schaik and Nederlandse Centrum voor Sensorische Integratie, *Cursus Manual Deel I-Somatosensory System* (Rotterdam, Netherlands: Haarlem/Transfer Groep, 2006).
4. Susan A. Greenfield, *The Human Mind Explained*, 1996.
5. Paul Madaule, *When Listening Comes Alive: A Guide to Effective Learning and Communication* (Ontario, Canada: Moulin Publishing, 1994).
6. Patricia A. Oetter, Eileen Richter, and Shelia Frick, *MORE: Integrating the Mouth with Sensory and Postural Functions.* (Stillmore, MN: PDP Products Inc., 1993), 1–10.
7. W. R. A. Oosterveld and Nederlandse Centrum voor Sensorische Integratie, *Cursus Manual Deel I-Vestibular System* (Rotterdam, Netherlands: Haarlem/Transfer Groep, 1990).
8. Patricia A. Oetter, Eileen Richter, and Shelia Frick, *MORE: Integrating the Mouth with Sensory and Postural Functions.*
9. H. Truby, "The Vestibular System, and the Sensory Systems of Smell and Taste," in *Principles of Neural Science* 3rd ed., eds. E. R. Kandel, J. H. Schwartz, and T. M. Jessell (Amsterdam, Netherlands: Elsevier, 1991), 512, 528, 500–510.
10. Carol Stock Kranowitz, *Out of Sync Child* (New York: Berkley, 1998).
11. A. Jean Ayres, *Sensory Integration and Learning Disorders* (Los Angeles: Western Psychological Services, 1972).
12. Carol Stock Kranowitz, *Out of Sync Child.*
13. Mary Kawar, *Refresher Course for SI Therapists* (Zandvoort, Netherlands: BEO Cursus, 2002). Course handout.
14. Chuck Murphy, *Je Zintuigen* [Your Senses] (Bussum, Holland: Van Reemst, 1981).
15. J. M. Fuster, "A Theory of Prefrontal Functions: The Prefrontal Cortex and the Temporal Organization of Behavior," in *The Prefrontal Cortex: Anatomy, Physiology, and Neuropsychology of the Frontal Lobe,* eds. George J. DuPaul and Gary Stoner, (New York: Raven Press, 1989), 1–15.
16. C. K. Conners, "Food Additives and Hyperkinesis: A Controlled Double-Blind Experiment," *Pediatrics* 58, no. 2 (1976): 154–166.
17. B. Feingold, "Why Your Child is Hyperactive," in *ADHD in the Schools,* eds. George J. DuPaul and Gary Stoner, New York: Guilford Press, 1994), 45–80.

18. Judith. G. Kimball, "Vestibular Stimulation and Seizure Activities," *Center for the Study of Sensory Integration Dysfunction Newsletter* (1976 July), 1–3.

Chapter 5

1. Lorna J. King, "Toward a Science of Adaptive Responses," *American Journal of Occupational Therapy* 32 (1978): 429–437.
2. A. Jean Ayres, *Sensory Integration and the Child* (Los Angeles: Western Psychological Services, 1980).
3. Lorna J. King, "Toward a Science of Adaptive Responses," 1978.
4. Judith G. Kimball, "The Emphasis is on Integration, Not Sensory," *American Journal of Mental Retardation* 92 (1988): 423–424.
5. Anne G. Fisher, Elizabeth A. Murray, and Anita C. Bundy, *Sensory Integration Theory and Practice*, 1991.
6. A. Jean Ayres, *Sensory Integration and Learning Disorders* (Los Angeles: Western Psychological Services, 1972).
7. A. Jean Ayres, *Sensory Integration and the Child.*
8. A. Jean Ayres, *Sensory Integration and Learning Disorders;* A. Jean Ayres, *Sensory Integration and the Child.*
9. Judith G. Kimball, "Vestibular Stimulation and Seizure Activities"; J. G. Kimball, "Case History Follow-up Report." *Dysfunction Center for the Study of Sensory Integration Newsletter* (1976 September), 1–3.
10. Mary Sue Williams and Sherry Shellenberger, *How Does Your Engine Run?* (Albuquerque, NM: Therapy Works, 1994).
11. Mary Sue Williams and Sherry Shellenberger, *How Does Your Engine Run?*
12. Patricia A. Oetter, "Treatment of Sensory Integration Dysfunction." Paper presented at Sensory Integration International, Los Angeles, CA, 10–12 September 1995).
13. Mary Kawar, *Refresher Course for SI Therapists* (Zandvoort, Netherlands: BEO Cursus, 2002). Course handout.

Chapter 6

1. Paul Madaule, *When Listening Comes Alive: A Guide to Effective Learning and Communication* (Ontario, Canada: Moulin Publishing, 1994).

Chapter 7

1. Lynn Horowitz, W. R. A. Oosterveld, and Ria Adrichem, "The Effectiveness of Sensory Integration Therapy on Ocular Pursuits and Organizational Time," *Pediatrics and Related Topics* 31, no. 5 (1993): 331–44.
2. Lynn Horowitz, "Dutch Pilot Study Test of Sensory Functions in Infants and Cultural Effect," paper presented at the World Federation of Occupational Therapists, London, 1994.
3. Lynn Horowitz and W. R. A. Duurkoop, "Pilot Study Presentation of Motor Observa-

tions," paper presented at the World Federation of Occupational Therapy, London, 1994.

Chapter 8

1. Lucy Jane Miller, *Sensational Kids* (Penguin, New York: 2006).
2. A. Jean Ayres, "Parent Questionnaire" presented at the "Introducing Sensory Integration Dysfunction and Therapy," symposium at Atlanta Speech School in Atlanta, GA, 1970; Patricia Wilbarger, "Parent Questionnaires for Sensory Integration Therapy," presented at Newest Scientific Developments Supporting Sensory Integration Therapy symposium at the Netherlands Center for Sensory Integration, Haarlem, Netherlands, 1980.

Glossary

adaptive response. the appropriate response—in movement or language—to a stimulus

ADD (Attention Deficit Disorder). attention problems

ADHD (Attention Deficit Hyperactivity Disorder). ADD with hyperactivity or excessive movement

arousal. the condition of the nervous system that determines at which rate a person is ready to receive information so he or she can pay attention in an appropriate manner

auditory. pertaining to hearing

central nervous system. the brain and the spinal cord

coordination. the fluent movement of muscles, in which all the senses play a role

eye movement. how the eyes move; for example, in order to follow an object

eye-hand coordination. the combination of eye-hand movements

fine motor skills. finer movements of the body, such as writing, coloring, fastening buttons, and tying shoelaces

modulation. a process to regulate how many stimuli the central nervous system can receive; regulation and adaptation of correct information occurs in coordination with the person's level of arousal and the situation

motor planning. how a new action is planned and organized

proprioception. unconscious information sent from the muscles, joints, and tendons to the brain concerning the state of the body while at rest and during movement

registration. the receiving of information by the brain and brain stem

senses. functions of the body that are involved in receiving stimuli from the body and the immediate environment

sensory integration. the ability to take in information about the immediate environment through the body, select information, and combine it to choose an appropriate reaction

tactile. pertaining to touch or the sensation of touch

tactile aversion. touch (i.e., possibly unexpected) that is experienced as unpleasant and something to avoid; for example, aversion to various clothing, textures, and even splashed water

tactile defensiveness. touch (i.e., possibly unexpected) that is experienced as unpleasant and threatening; the person may be annoyed or react in a negative fashion or defensively

tone. muscle tone, tension in the muscles

vestibular. equilibrium sensory system that helps with balance, reaction to gravity, and ability to keep eyes on a target while the person is moving

visual. information that is received through the eyes, processed in the brain, and then coordinated with other sensory systems for a person to understand the information appropriately.

Additional References

American Psychiatric Association (APA). 1994. *Diagnostic and Statistical Manual of Mental Disorders.* 4th ed. Washington, DC: APA.

Beery, Keith E. 1997. *The Beery-Buktenica Developmental Test of Visual-motor Integration.* 4th ed. Parsippany, NJ: Modern Curriculum Press.

Cool, Stephen. J. 1995. Does sensory integration work? *Sensory Integration Quarterly* 23, no. 1 (Summer): 1–8.

Diagram Group. 1983. *The Brain: A User's Manual.* New York: Berkley.

Dunn, Winifred. 1997. The impact of sensory processing abilities on the daily lives of young children and their families: A conceptual model. *Infants and Young Children* 9, no. 4:23–24.

Fisher, Anne G., Elizabeth A. Murray, and Anita C. Bundy. 1991. *Sensory Integration Theory and Practice.* Philadelphia, PA: Davis.

Forssberg, Hans. 2002. Deficit in sensory-motor integration in clumsy children. *Symposium: The Clumsy Child, Aetiology, Pathogenesis and Treatment* (6–8 June) 41.

Hellerstein, Lynn F., and Beth I. Fishman. 1999. Collaboration between occupational therapists and optometrists. *Journal of Behavioral Optometry* 10, no. 6:2–3.

Heiniger, Margot. C., and Shirley. L. Randolph. 1981. *Neurophysiological Concepts in Human Behavior: The Tree of Learning.* St. Louis, MO: C.V. Mosby.

Kandel, E. R., J. H. Schwartz, and T. M. Jessell. *Principles of Neural Science.* 3rd ed. 481–498, 500–510, Amsterdam, Netherlands: Elsevier.

Leach, Penelope. 1978. *Your Baby and Child from Birth to Age Five.* New York: Knopf.

Njiokiktjien, Charles. 1988. *Pediatric Behavioral Neurology: Clinical Principles.* Vol. 1. Amsterdam, Netherlands: Suyi Publishing.

Pulaski, Mary Ann Spencer. 1978. *Your Baby's Mind and How It Grows: Piaget's Theory for Parents.* London, UK: Cassel.

Schoenmaker, M. M. 2002. *Physiotherapy in Clumsy Children.* Paper presented at The Clumsy Child: Aetiology, Pathogenesis and Treatment in Groningen, Netherlands (6–8 June).

Solomons, H. 1978. *Binocular Vision: A Programmed Text*. London, UK: Heineman Medical Books.

Yack, E. 1989. Sensory integration: A survey of its use in the clinical setting. *Canadian Journal of Occupational Therapy* 56, no. 5:229–235.

Resources

Suitable terms to use in search engines include ADHD, hyperactivity, attention, sensory integration, sensory integration therapy, and sensory processing disorder.

www.crestport.com
This small publishing house has a book entitled *With Love, From Jean,* which features Dr. A. Jean Ayres's letters to her nephew and which is especially touching and illuminating. She gives advice by mail and discusses her views about SI therapy as it was in its earliest stages.

www.integrationscatalog.com
This website has a large selection of books and therapeutic materials, including materials especially designed for full environments. It also has a parent chat room and educational sessions. The owner has a private practice in the Orlando, Florida area.

www.jumpin@chartermi.net
This website lists courses for professionals, and its catalogue includes an extensive list of therapeutic products. The owner has a private practice in the Ann Arbor, Michigan, area and offers SI therapy, metronome, and cranial sacral interventions.

www.kidfoundation.org
This foundation was originally geared toward research and continues to promote research in many areas related to SI. The foundation is active in promoting the name sensory processing disorders, with the goal of obtaining a DSM listing. The website has a large parent-professional network.

http://medlineplus.gov
Medlineplus is the website of the U.S. National Library of Medicine and the National Institutes of Health. You can find an overview of recent articles if you search using such terms as hyperactivity and children. Short summaries of research articles are accessible on the website.

www.pediatrictherapynetwork.org
This website lists information about its Los Angeles, California area therapy center. It has developmental information and chat rooms and has plans for a listing of therapists.

www.sensoryint.com
Sensory Integration International (SII) is the original organization for parents and thera-

pists set up by Dr. A. Jean Ayres and Patricia Wilbarger, M.A., FAOTA. A listing of SI courses is available as well as copies of previous newsletters, books, and pamphlets.

www.sensoryresources.com
This website offers information about workshops, meetings, and publications.

www.sierf.org
This is the website of the Sensory Integration Education and Research Foundation. Two occupational therapists and the parent of a child with SI problems set up this organization. It provides support and education, and it distributes information about SI to parents and professionals. This website offers book reviews and chat rooms.

www.sifocus.com
S.I. Focus magazine is an international magazine about SI that is written for parents and professionals. The website offers announcements about courses and parent groups in the Dallas area.

www.SInetwork.org
This website contains a list of SI-trained therapists in England, Ireland, Scotland, and other countries. It also has a very well-written newsletter that includes course information and tips for setting up a discussion group for parents.

www.sensationalkids.org
This website is part of the Kid Foundation web network. It is specifically geared to announcing the new book *Sensational Kids* by Dr. Lucy Miller. It includes important information about the new name, sensory processing disorders.

www.STARcenter.us.org
This is a large private practice, offering music therapies for auditory disorders (as well as for sensory integration/sensory processing disorders), parent support groups, and educational services. It is located in the Denver, Colorado, area.

www.southpawenterprises.com
This website features an equipment catalog for SI therapy and has a very fine selection of books for parents and professionals.

www.TherapySkillBuilder.com *or* www.PsychCorp.com
This website primarily offers books, videos, and therapeutic training programs for special-needs children and adults.

www.VitalLinks.net *and* Vitalsounds.com
This website lists information and products about therapeutic listening and other auditory interventions, SI products, books, and courses. The owners have a private practice in Madison, Wisconsin.

Index

404 DESKSIDE ACTIVITIES FOR ENERGETIC
KIDS *by Barbara Davis, M.S., MFA*

This invaluable resource helps K–3 teachers deal with restless students who may otherwise disrupt the class. It describes short movement breaks that can be used between other classroom activities to maintain a positive learning environment. It begins with activities for developing motor skills and alphabet recognition, and moves through progressively more complex skills.

Contents include

— stretching and relaxing movements, shaking and waking-up movements, pantomime
— complex movement games, including improv, rhythm and clapping, balancing, and team relays

The activities are marked according to age levels, time of play, and group size. No activity requires special skills, and there are enough for every day of the school year.

◆ 168 pages ... Paperback $14.95 ... Spiral bound $19.95

101 LIFE SKILLS GAMES FOR CHILDREN: LEARNING, GROWING, GETTING ALONG (AGES 6–12)

by Bernie Badegruber

How do you teach children tolerance and responsibility or help them deal with fear, mistrust, or aggression? Play a Life Skills game with them! Games are an ideal way to help children learn emotional and social skills; for example, how to integrate the new girl into the group, how to cope with aggression and group conflict, and safe ways to let off steam.

◆ 192 pages ... Paperback $14.95 ... Spiral bound $19.95

101 MOVEMENT GAMES FOR CHILDREN: Fun and Learning with Playful Movement
by Huberta Wiertsema

Movement games help children develop sensory awareness, ease of movement, and using movement for self-expression. Games are organized into sections including reaction games, cooperation games, and expression games, and include variations on old favorites such as Duck, Duck, Goose as well as new games such as Equal Pacing and Moving Joints.

◆ 160 pages ... Paperback $14.95 ... Spiral bound $19.95

101 IMPROV GAMES FOR CHILDREN AND ADULTS *by Bob Bedore*

Improv comedy has become wildly popular, and this book offers the next step in drama and play skills: a guide to creating something out of nothing and reaching out to people using talents you didn't know you possessed. Contains instructions and exercises for teaching improv to children, advanced improv techniques, and tips for thinking on your feet—all from an acknowledged master of the improv form.

◆ 192 pages ... Paperback $14.95 ... Spiral bound $19.95

42 MANDALA PATTERNS
COLORING BOOK *by Wolfgang Hund*

A perfect introduction to the joy of coloring mandalas, the designs in this book mix traditional and modern themes, and nature elements such as trees and stars with animals such as fish, doves, and butterflies. Motifs repeat within mandalas in a soothing way, and we can find new shapes and meanings in them each time.

◆ 96 pages ... 42 illus. ... Paperback $11.95

42 INDIAN MANDALAS
COLORING BOOK *by Monika Helwig*

Traditionally, mandalas such as the ones in this book have been used to decorate homes, temples, and meeting places for centuries. They may be used daily as well as on special occasions, and they are found in the homes of people of all faiths. Each pattern is different and special.

◆ 96 pages ... 42 illus. ... Paperback $11.95

42 SEASONAL MANDALAS
COLORING BOOK *by Wolfgang Hund*

The seasonal and holiday mandalas in this book will appeal to both the sophisticated and the primal in all of us. Fruit, flowers, leaves, and snowflakes are among the nature designs. Holiday themes include bunnies and jack-o-lanterns, Christmas scenes, and New Year's noisemakers. Children can learn about seasons and celebrate familiar holidays with these playful designs!

◆ 96 pages ... 42 illus. ... Paperback $11.95

CPSIA information can be obtained
at www.ICGtesting.com
Printed in the USA
LVOW09s0105011217
558247LV00003B/54/P